Why Not the Best?

ALSO IN THE CARTER COLLECTION

A Government as Good as Its People

The Blood of Abraham
Insights into the Middle East

An Outdoor Journal
Adventures and Reflections

First Lady from Plains

Keeping Faith
Memoirs of a President

Everything to Gain
Making the Most of the Rest of Your Life

Why Not the Best?

Jimmy Carter

The First Fifty Years

WITH AN INTRODUCTION
BY DOUGLAS BRINKLEY

The University of Arkansas Press
Fayetteville • 1996

06   05   04   03   02   5   4   3   2

Designed by Ellen Beeler

☉ The paper used in this publication meets the minimum requirements of the
American National Standard for Permanence of Paper for Printed Library Materials
Z39.48-1984.

Library of Congress Cataloging-in-Publication Data

Carter, Jimmy, 1924–
    Why not the best? : the first fifty years / Jimmy Carter : with an introduction by
Doug Brinkley.
        p.   cm.
    Originally published: Nashville : Broadman Press, 1975.
    ISBN 1-55728-418-0 (p : alk. paper)
    1. Carter, Jimmy, 1924–   . 2. Governors—Georgia—Biography. 3. Presidents—
United States—Biography. I. Title.
E873.A3   1996
973.926'092—dc20
    [B]   96-17579
                                                                             CIP

Acknowledgment is made for use of quoted material on page ix.

From "The Hand That Signed the Paper." Copyright 1939. From *The Poems of Dylan
Thomas*. New York: New Directions Publishing Corporation. Reprinted by permission
of New Directions Publishing Corporation.

From "Song to Woody," Words and Music by Bob Dylan. Copyright 1962, 1965, by
Duchess Music Corporation, 445 Park Avenue, New York, New York 10022. Used by
permission. All rights reserved.

Photographs are from the Charles M. Rafshoon Photographs Collection in the Special
Collections Department, Robert W. Woodruff Library, Emory University. They include
reproductions of Carter family photos as well as other photos taken by Mr. Rafshoon
and used with his permission.

Dedicated to my mother, Lillian,
and my wife, Rosalynn

Contents

The sad duty of politics is to establish justice in a sinful world.

—Reinhold Neibuhr

Hey, hey, Woody Guthrie, I wrote you a song
'Bout a funny ol' world that's a-comin' along.
Seems sick an' it's hungry, it's tired and it's torn,
It looks like it's a-dyin' an' it's hardly been born.

—Bob Dylan

Great is the hand that holds dominion over
Man by a scribbled name.
The five kings count the dead but do not soften
The crusted wound nor stroke the brow;
A hand rules pity as a hand rules heaven;
Hands have no tears to flow.

—Dylan Thomas

Introduction

"Tell me the landscape in which you live, and I will tell you who you are."
                                        —José Ortega Gassett

In late 1974 when Georgia governor Jimmy Carter's presidential ambitions were not taken seriously by the national media, he began writing a campaign autobiography that was instrumental in helping him capture the White House. With nearly one million copies eventually sold, *Why Not the Best?* convinced many skeptics that this eighth-generation Georgian was the best candidate to lead America into its third century. To a public still coming to terms with the Vietnam War and Watergate, Carter's soothing memoir was a welcome affirmation of one candidate's bedrock faith in old-fashioned public service based on duty, honor, competence, and honesty. Anyone who read Carter's personal history could not fail to be moved by the images he painted of his idyllic childhood in remote Plains, his hazing incident at Annapolis for refusing to sing "Marching through Georgia," his near-death experience aboard a Pacific-fleet submarine and his born-again religious experience, the compassionate humor of his mother, Miss Lillian, and the stern taskmaster ethics of his father, Mr. Earl. In compelling yet humble language, *Why Not the Best?* introduced the world to the remarkable talents and ambitious humanity of Jimmy Carter.

The idea of writing a campaign autobiography was first presented to Jimmy Carter by his twenty-seven-year-old political strategist Hamilton Jordan in a prophetic seventy-page memorandum dated November 4, 1972, the day before Richard Nixon's landslide victory over George McGovern in the presidential election. The memo, Carter's game plan to win the presidential nomination in 1976, included the arduous task of writing a memoir to introduce himself to the voters. "It seems not to have occurred to him that most candidates let others celebrate them," Gary Wills wrote about the book in an otherwise favorable *Atlantic* profile. But Jimmy Carter was not like "most candidates"—it was his unorthodox approach to politics that made him so appealing in the first place.

Unlike other presidential autobiographies, *Why Not the Best?* was written entirely by Carter, with some editorial assistance provided by Hal Gulliver, the associate editor of the *Atlanta Journal-Constitution*. Carter had read James David Barber's book *Presidential Character* (1972), from which he learned that a politician's style and purpose are expressed most truthfully in the early chapters of an autobiography: the lessons retained from youth. Carter knew that in this regard his rural Plains upbringing, peanut-farmer existence, distinguished naval career, and New South business perspective could set him apart from the Washington-style Democratic contenders. He was the rare politician, one without a single skeleton in his closet. So what if he was the proverbial outsider, never having fought in the political trenches along with other national Democrats in the great battles of the era—the Vietnam War, Medicaid and Medicare, civil-rights legislation, Nixon's Supreme Court appointments, Watergate. This could be an asset, not a liability. "The best politics is to do the best job yourself," Carter would note. "And I put my best foot forward when writing *Why Not the Best?*"

Throughout the late summer of 1974 Governor Carter shopped his book idea around to publishing firms to no avail. Unsure of how next to proceed he asked Hal Gulliver for tactical help. "A short (1–100 pg.) well-written book that you obviously wrote is worth much more (both to you and a publisher) than will be some extensive book that sounds like it was written by staff or other writers," Gulliver advised. With still no bites, Carter used his considerable pull as a member of the Southern Baptist's Brotherhood Commission to cut a deal with Broadman Press in Nashville, with whom he had planned to write an evangelical tract. (Broadman Press was an "inspirational literature" house, dealing strictly in books, audiovisuals, and music celebrating the life of Jesus Christ.)

A straightforward autobiography about Jimmy Carter's multifaceted life, Gulliver insisted, was what the voting public would want to read. A religious book marketed solely to America's twenty million Baptists would not have a broad enough appeal for a serious presidential candidate, especially one with low name recognition. Eventually abandoning the notion of writing both books at once, Carter went with Gulliver's editorial instinct and began the autobiography. He made it clear from the outset, however, that spiritual themes would pervade his memoir, since praying was, as he once put it, "like breathing to me." Broadman Press assigned Joe Jackson to be Carter's editor, a born-again book novice who would eventually sign his correspondence to the one-term governor with "All the *BEST* to you and Rosalynn."

Hal Gulliver, writing for the *Atlanta Journal-Constitution*, had heard dozens of Jimmy Carter yarns over the years as he covered the self-assured peanut farmer's meteoric political rise from the Sumter County Board of Education to the governor's mansion. The Admiral Hyman Rickover "Why Not the Best?" story—which Carter had recently used to great effect at the National Press Club where on December 12, 1974, he had formally announced his presidential candidacy—stood out in his mind as the most memorable, and he urged Carter to consider using it as both the title and the introduction.

Carter conceded to Gulliver on the Rickover opening and, of course, did call his book *Why Not the Best?* Besides reflecting the lesson he carried away from his job interview with Rickover when he was applying for the nuclear submarine program, the title also reflected Carter's self-confident nature as he tried to convince people that he was going to win the Democratic presidential nomination. The homiletic message was that Jimmy Carter was the candidate best suited to be president.

As Carter envisioned it, his book would be less an overt appeal for votes and more the story of one righteous Southerner's coming of age, with James Agee's *Let Us Now Praise Famous Men*, Hyman Rickover's *Eminent Americans*, and Carl Sandburg's *Abraham Lincoln: The Prairie Years and the War Years*, as stylistic models. Realizing that he was unequipped to write elaborately beautiful prose like Thomas Wolfe, Carter would settle for something more in line with the smooth, finely crafted efforts of the New Jersey essayist John McPhee, whose entire body of work he had devoured. "I need your frank suggestions and believe I'm capable of taking them," Carter wrote Gulliver on October 17, 1974, in a letter accompanied by drafts of his first two chapters. "I tend to write like an engineer and save words. Can expand any parts you indicate, or change tone. Will be working on another while I wait to hear from you."

One way he thought to showcase his unique qualities, and to demonstrate to Kennedy-McGovern liberals and *Rolling Stone* aficionados that being an evangelical did not mean you were a brainwashed square, was to place personally meaningful quotations at the beginning of the autobiography to debunk the notion that all rural Southerners were hillbilly characters from TV's "Hee Haw." The Reinhold Niebuhr maxim—"The sad duty of politics is to establish justice in a sinful world"—was at the top of the list. In thirteen words Carter's favorite neo-orthodox theologian had succinctly summed up his own rationale for seeking the White House.

Carter also wanted to display, particularly for a younger audience, his affinity for folk singer Bob Dylan. Although his taste ran to classical music, especially Wagner and Shostakovich, Carter had been moved by the pure poetry of Dylan's lyrics, which all three of his twenty-something sons played at home with steadfast devotion. So, as his boys wore out the grooves of *The Times They Are a Changin'*, Carter absorbed songs such as "The Lonesome Death of Hattie Carrol" and "The Ballad of Hollis Brown," laments on the injustices suffered by the poor and disadvantaged. The impact that Dylan's songs and Niebuhr's theology had on Carter's consciousness is revealed in a remarkable speech he delivered on Law Day at the University of Georgia in 1974: "One of the sources of my understanding about the proper applications of criminal justice and the system of equity is from Reinhold Niebuhr. The other source of my understanding about what's right and wrong in this society is from a friend of mine, a poet named Bob Dylan."

Carter eventually summed up the gist of Dylan's sentiment in *Why Not the Best?*: "I have always looked on the presidency of the United States with reverence and awe, and I still do. But recently I have begun to realize that the president is just a human being." The point here being that Jimmy Carter, unlike the other big shots seeking the White House, was an authentic man of the people, not a puppet of vested interest. After a personal tug-of-war, Carter chose the populist verse from "Song for Woody," the only original song on Dylan's first album, because it was concise, had a universalist message, and was compatible with the Niebuhr quote. The Dylan Thomas poem went through the same sort of careful consideration, with five verses in the running before a poignant selection from "The Hand That Signed the Paper" was made.

Carter wrote to Joe Jackson at Broadman Press in March 1975 with a list of rough chapter outlines, the titles of which sounded like songs on a Bob Dylan album: "I Ain't Nobody," "Once I Was Old; Now I Am Younger," and "Don't Look Ahead" (instead of Dylan's "Don't Look Back"). The other proposed chapter titles illuminated Carter's interest in Dylan Thomas and presaged his own verse, which would be published twenty years later as *Always A Reckoning* (1995): "No Thanks in the Lord's Prayer," "Governors Are Not Unemployed," "Kiss for a Leprous Child," "Legal But Wrong," and "A Church with 80,000 Members." His chapter on nuclear defense issues was to be called "We Can Kill Them 37 Times"; on preventive health care, "Let's Stamp Out Typhoid"; and on the civil-rights movement, "Who Got the Struggle?"

A close look at the original drafts of *Why Not the Best?*, housed at the Jimmy Carter Presidential Library in Atlanta, offers a fascinating window into the mindset and campaign strategy of the first politician south of the Mason-Dixie line to capture the White House in his own right since Zachary Taylor in 1848. Working on yellow scratch pads and desk stationery while crisscrossing the nation trying to muster support for his presidential candidacy, Carter would bring his travel scrawl home to Plains on weekends to edit in his office den. Not wanting to waste good paper, he typed his first draft on the back of discarded State of Georgia Executive Department letterhead with "Jimmy Carter • Governor" printed on the left-hand corner and "Hamilton Jordan • Executive Secretary" on the right.

That March of 1975 Carter was hurriedly pounding away on his portable typewriter, frustrated that campaign obligations in forty states prevented him from making the book a priority. Carter's media advisor Gerald Rafshoon and campaign manager

Hamilton Jordan were worried that their man was squandering too much precious campaign time perfecting *Why Not the Best?* They watched in dismay as Carter struggled to conjure the right phrase or image while composing at a motel desk in Texas or on a Delta flight en route to Washington. The frustration that all conscientious authors feel when the appropriate word eludes them tortured Carter, a stubborn perfectionist, as his May manuscript delivery deadline hovered over him. "If I hadn't given up drinking for the campaign we could do much better," he joked to Gulliver. For besides being a perfectionist, Carter was also a punctualist, adopting from his naval years the notion that being even a minute tardy for anything was unacceptable. Come hell or high water, Broadman Press would have his final version of *Why Not the Best?* on schedule.

Scrapping all the fancy Dylanesque chapter titles for minimalist ones—"Farm," "Military," and "Governor"—Carter shifted himself into high gear, cutting and pasting, marking up pages with word balloons and insert arrows, crossing out some of his oversentimental "daddy's" for the more highbrow "father" when referring to Mr. Earl, replacing the possibly offensive "jews' harp" for the more politically correct "small piccolo" when listing musical instruments classmates played at Plains High School. At last the text—which was known among Carterites as "The Red Book," due to the color of the manuscript folder—was approaching the desirable final form. "Ah, ole friend, I speak the truth," Gulliver wrote Carter on March 23 after reading his chapter drafts. "The book is shaping up as maybe being very good, as I hoped it might be, and I had high hopes from the first day after we talked about it."

By mid-April Carter sent *Why Not the Best?* to his campaign treasurer, lawyer Bob Lipshutz, along with Rafshoon and Gulliver, for final critical review before officially shipping it off to Nashville. They were all impressed. Appropriate photographs were quickly gathered to accompany the text, including the all-important workingman shots with Carter hauling and shoveling peanuts. If you couldn't trust a farmer, whom could you trust? *Why Not the Best?* struck just the right chord. Jimmy Carter had created an inspired work of original literature that transcended the tired campaign-book genre. Its open-minded, Christian appeal was unlike anything that had come down the nearly two-hundred-year-old pike of American presidential politics. Carter had achieved his objective: a thoughtful potpourri of a Main Street memoir anchored by his no-nonsense style and homespun storytelling.

Carter had done his job well: *Why Not the Best?* offered something for everyone. It was now time for his campaign staff to earn its keep. Acting as Carter's lawyer, Lipshutz (of the Atlanta firm Lipshutz, Macey, Zusmann, and Skies) sent Broadman Press back their contract accompanied by a new one he had drafted himself. Lipshutz made it clear that Carter was less interested in making money than in receiving maximum exposure for *Why Not the Best?* After all, Lipshutz noted, Carter had written the autobiography to promote his candidacy for U.S. president. Demands were made, and met, for Broadman Press to take out advertisements in fourteen different newspapers including the *New York Times* and the *Christian Science Monitor,* as well as every conceivable Baptist publication. With *Why Not the Best?* prominently displayed in bookstores, the enigmatic "Jimmy Who?" would soon evaporate, replaced by "Jimmy Everyman": Southerner, husband, father, peanut farmer, nuclear physicist, bible teacher, politician, businessman, hunter, engineer, environmentalist, "lover of Bob Dylan's songs and Dylan Thomas's poetry," and soon to be best-selling author.

The promotional strategy paid off big. Broadman Press released *Why Not the Best?* on Carter's birthday, October 1, right in time for the Christmas market and five months before the all-important New Hampshire primary on February 24. Joe Jackson scarcely had cause to blue-pencil the manuscript, save mending split infinitives and adding forgotten commas.

There had been no advance money extended to Carter, but Broadman Press had agreed to give him a few thousand hardback copies of *Why Not the Best?* as payment. No sooner had the boxes arrived at his Plains peanut warehouse than Jimmy and Rosalynn Carter began handing out complimentary copies to potential supporters and national journalists; others were sold for five dollars at early political rallies. Georgia friends such as John and Betty Pope of Americus took with them hundreds of autographed copies of

Why Not the Best? for the "Peanut Brigaders" to distribute as they canvassed door-to-door in snow-covered New Hampshire towns to promote the relatively unknown former governor.

The book had an electrifying effect in the New Hampshire and Iowa primaries. People who read *Why Not the Best?* became devoted to Carter's outsider candidacy. No matter one's political predilection, it was nearly impossible not to like the man portrayed in the book. David Garst, an Iowa agribusinessman who had never supported anyone in a presidential race before, went to work for Carter after reading *Why Not the Best?*, raising fifty thousand dollars for him as a matter of conscience. Actor Robert Redford recommended the book on radio talk shows. A Manchester, New Hampshire, physician purchased two hundred copies to give to friends for New Year's gifts. The Allman Brothers Band had fans read passages aloud at one of their rock concerts. A handful of civics teachers in Des Moines assigned it for extra-credit reading in their high-school courses. As unlikely as it might seem, *Why Not the Best?* made Carter "hip." Since the central focus of Carter's populist campaign was the persona of Jimmy Carter, his book complemented him, becoming the indispensable guidebook to the man who would become America's thirty-ninth president.

To the surprise of most pollsters and media analysts, who, ever since the Kennedy-Nixon debates of 1960, believed that the selling of a president had to take place on television, *Why Not the Best?* rocketed up the bestseller list. A senior editor at Little Brown who had rejected the book idea a year earlier, despite Gulliver's pleas, later recalled his decision as one of the two biggest mistakes of his professional career (the other being turning down Peter Benchley's *Jaws*). By the time Carter defeated Governor George Wallace of Alabama in the Florida primary, almost assuring himself the Democratic nomination, Broadman Press could not churn out hardback editions at a fast enough clip to meet the public demand. Bantam Books of New York hustled to fill the void, issuing a handsome paperback edition that sold out so quickly that they were compelled to print a new edition every couple of weeks. At the Democratic National Convention in Madison Square Garden that July, many dedicated delegates clutched their dog-eared copy of *Why Not the Best?* as if it were divine scripture. To some, the book alone was enough to cause them to vote for Carter.

Moreover, every writer who wanted to file a "personal" story on Jimmy Carter had to read between the lines of *Why Not the Best?* Almost as a matter of policy Carter would ask reporters about to interview him if they had read his book. The *New Yorker's* Elizabeth Drew tells the story of riding in a town car with Carter in March of 1976 between Chicago stump speeches. When Drew dared to ask Carter if he had a master plan for his campaign, he snapped, "It's in the book . . . how I decided to run for the presidency, and the plans are in the book. There's no point in our talking about these things when they're in the book." Taken aback, Drew explained that Gerald Rafshoon was attempting to locate a copy for her. An agitated Carter replied, "It's in the stores."

Any wise Democrat hoping to be employed as a member of a future Carter administration memorized vignettes from *Why Not the Best?* to tell at social gatherings as proof that Jimmy Carter was, if not the second coming of FDR or JFK, awfully close. Vice-presidential hopefuls from Henry "Scoop" Jackson to Edmund Muskie told reporters that *Why Not the Best?* was a tremendous literary device for winning the White House. Walter Mondale went one giant leap further. When asked by a reporter about how he prepared for his vice-presidential interview with Carter, Mondale answered: "The first thing I did was read the most remarkable book ever written, called *Why Not the Best?* I found every word absolutely brilliant." Mondale got the job.

It would be a disservice to overstate the importance that *Why Not the Best?* played in Carter's electoral victory over Gerald Ford in November 1976. Once Carter had won his party's nomination, the book became more of a memorable souvenir than required reading. But this is only because Carter's portrayal of his life had already fully ingrained itself in the nation's psyche. Carter's Plains, Georgia, had become as symbolic as Truman's Independence, Missouri, or Lincoln's Springfield, Illinois. Salted peanuts and green-and-white Carter-Mondale bumper stickers had become the rage. Miss Lillian was a household celebrity; Rosalynn was the toast-of-the-town. Ray Charles's version of "Georgia on My Mind" was getting more AM radio airplay than the Beatles and Beach Boys combined. Almost overnight Jimmy Carter had become the stuff of legend. The public hoped that the author of *Why Not the Best?* would usher in a new era of responsive and responsible government.

The Jimmy Carter saga does not, of course, end in 1976. Candidate Carter became President Carter only to be relegated to Citizen Carter four years later. Those four years were not easy ones, but with the perspective of time such notable achievements as SALT II, the Panama Canal treaties, the Alaska Lands Act, the Camp David accords, the successful release of the fifty-two American hostages held captive in Iran, an activist human-rights agenda, the normalization of relations with China, his advocacy of majority rule in Africa, and many other important policy initiatives will trigger a favorable reappraisal of his administration. Carter will go down in history as a very good, if sometimes politically naive, president. Over twenty years after the publication of *Why Not the Best?*, it is clear that Carter did fulfill his campaign promises: never to lie to the American people and to bring integrity back to the White House.

After losing to Ronald Reagan in the 1980 presidential election, Carter took it upon himself to write a second book, a memoir of his White House years entitled *Keeping Faith*. Carter signed the contract for this book at a private dinner at Morven, the official home of then–New Jersey governor Brendon Byrne, who served as his witness, while John McPhee performed the same role for Bantam publishers. Carter was in the Garden State to consult with scholars of the presidency, particularly with the distinguished American historian Arthur Link, editor of the Woodrow Wilson papers. "In preparation for his visit, I read his previous autobiography, *Why Not the Best?*," Link recalled. "It's a marvelous book, particularly the early chapters, and I recommended that he try to maintain that pure and honest storytelling tone." Carter left Princeton ready to write, and write he did.

Since 1981—besides assuming the role as our nation's finest ex-president and most acclaimed international peacemaker— Jimmy Carter has become the best-selling author of over half a dozen titles. Whether he was writing about his presidency in

Keeping Faith, life as an activist senior citizen in *Everything to Gain* (coauthored with Rosalynn), the virtues of conservationism in *An Outdoor Journal*, his early political career in *Turning Point*, or presenting his populist poems in *Always a Reckoning*, the bittersweet virtues of Plains first evoked in *Why Not the Best?* are always present. Carter's social photograph of his hometown is a realistic portrait that illuminates the hamlet's commitment to civic virtues. The publication of *Why Not the Best?*, along with Carter's presidential candidacy, helped make Main Street popular again at the very moment when cynicism had become the national pastime.

Now that the political relevance of *Why Not the Best?* has dissipated, one can view Carter's sparse prose through a less partisan lens, discovering the vulnerable poetry that was always hidden by the more potent political message. Today when reading his first book, one is disarmed by introspective lines such as "Sometimes I felt lonesome and timid as a small salesman" or "I stayed up alone sometimes, after everyone else was asleep, to listen to Glenn Miller while lying on the floor in front of the fireplace." While never nostalgic, Carter has a gift for sentiment. His descriptive ability is especially apparent when discussing farm life and related childhood activities: "Our toys were found or made on the farm. We rolled steel barrel hoops with a heavy wire pusher, slid down pine-straw hills on old disc plow blades, hunted with sling shots and flips, flew homemade kites and June bugs on a string, and threw spinning projectiles made of corncobs and chicken feathers."

Reading *Why Not the Best?* reminds us, in the same way that building a house for Habitat for Humanity with Jimmy Carter does, that this Georgian's entire life has brimmed with moral purpose and genuine accomplishment. Now that the 1976 presidential campaign has faded into memory, his autobiography can be enjoyed as the inspirational book Broadman Press always knew it to be. Jimmy Carter's *Why Not the Best?*, on any number of levels, is like its author—a national treasure.

Douglas Brinkley
Director of the Eisenhower Center
University of New Orleans

I had applied for the nuclear submarine program, and Admiral Rickover was interviewing me for the job. It was the first time I met Admiral Rickover, and we sat in a large room by ourselves for more than two hours, and he let me choose any subjects I wished to discuss. Very carefully, I chose those about which I knew most at the time—current events, seamanship, music, literature, naval tactics, electronics, gunnery—and he began to ask me a series of questions of increasing difficulty. In each instance, he soon proved that I knew relatively little about the subject I had chosen.

He always looked right into my eyes, and he never smiled. I was saturated with cold sweat.

Finally, he asked me a question and I thought I could redeem myself. He said, "How did you stand in your class at the Naval Academy?" Since I had completed my sophomore year at Georgia Tech before entering Annapolis as a plebe, I had done very well, and I swelled my chest with pride and answered, "Sir, I stood fifty-ninth in a class of 820!" I sat back to wait for the congratulations—which never came. Instead, the question: "Did you do your best?" I started to say, 'Yes, sir," but I remembered who this was, and recalled several of the many times at the Academy when I could have learned more about our allies, our enemies, weapons, strategy, and so forth. I was just human. I finally gulped and said, "No, sir, I didn't always do my best."

He looked at me for a long time, and then turned his chair around to end the interview. He asked one final question, which I have never been able to forget—or to answer. He said, "Why not?" I sat there for a while, shaken, and then slowly left the room.

ONE

Two Questions

As we observe the two hundredth birthday of our nation, it is appropriate to ask ourselves two basic questions:

Can our government be honest, decent, open, fair, and compassionate?

Can our government be competent?

As a matter of fact, many millions of American citizens have been asking these questions and are doubtful about whether either can be answered in the affirmative.

The tragedies of Cambodia and Vietnam, the shock, embarrassment, and shame of Watergate, the doubt and confusion surrounding the economic woes of our nation—these have created unprecedented doubt and soul-searching among our people.

Does our government in Washington now represent accurately what the American people are or what we ought to be? The answer is clearly, "No!"

Can our government in Washington represent accurately what the American people are or what we ought to be? The answer to this second question is sought throughout this book.

This is an autobiographical book, written by one who is still actively involved in politics. But it is not a political autobiography. It is written as a kind of summing up of my opinions about our nation—based on my own observations and experiences. It is written, too, in the belief that these personal experiences have relevance to the values most Americans want to see embraced at the top levels of our national leadership.

Within our free society each of us has an opportunity to develop a wide range of abilities, characteristics, responsibilities, and interests. I am a Southerner and an American. I am a farmer, an engineer, a father and husband, a Christian, a politician and former governor, a planner, a businessman, a nuclear physicist, a naval officer, a canoeist, and, among other things, a lover of Bob Dylan's songs and Dylan Thomas's poetry.

As the philosopher Sören Kierkegaard said, "Every man is an exception." We Americans are proud of such individuality and diversity. But we still share common dreams. Neither Vietnam, nor Watergate, nor the hardships of a mismanaged economy can change that.

Some of our shared dreams are easy to state, if not always so easy to achieve. They include the beliefs that all Americans should stand equal before the law, that our country should, among the community of nations, set an example of courage, compassion, honor, and dedication to basic human rights and freedoms, and that government should be controlled by our citizens and not the other way around. Some of our dreams are more subtle, more difficult to put into words.

We must remember that our nation still retains its own inherent greatness. Our inherent economic strength, our natural resources, and our human resources are certainly no less than they were two years ago, or two decades ago, or two centuries ago.

The proper tapping of this reservoir of strength, courage, and ability is the joint responsibility of all of us, and particularly as we consider the bicentennial of our nation.

On September 5, 1974, I met with the governors of the other twelve original states in Philadelphia. It was exactly two hundred years after the convening of the First Continental Congress when we walked down those same historic streets, then turned left, and entered a small building named Carpenter's Hall. There we listened to the same prayer and sat in the same chairs occupied in 1774 by Samuel Adams, John Jay, John Adams, Patrick Henry, George Washington, and about forty-five other strong and often opinionated leaders.

Those first leaders of what would become the United States

held widely divergent views, and they debated for furious weeks. They and others who joined them for the Second Continental Congress avoided the production of timid compromise resolutions. They were somehow inspired, and they reached for greatness. Their written premises formed the basis on which our nation was begun.

I don't know whose particular chair I occupied that day in Philadelphia but, sitting there, I thought soberly about their times two centuries ago and ours of the 1970s. Their people were also discouraged, disillusioned, and confused. But these early leaders acted with purpose and conviction.

I wondered to myself, were they more competent, more intelligent, or better educated than we? Were they more courageous? Did they love their land more? Did they have more compassion or concern for their neighbors? Did they have deeper religious convictions? Were they more interested in the future of their children than we?

I think not.

We Americans today are equally capable of correcting our faults, overcoming difficulties, managing our own affairs, and facing the future with justifiable confidence. I am convinced that among us 213,000,000 Americans there is a willingness and even eagerness to restore in our country what has been lost—*if* we have understandable purposes and goals and a modicum of bold and inspired leadership.

Our government can express the highest common ideals of human beings—*if* we demand of government true standards of excellence. At this bicentennial time of introspection and concern, we must demand such standards.

It is now time to stop and to ask ourselves the question which my last commanding officer, Admiral Hyman Rickover, asked me and every other young naval officer in the atomic submarine program.

Why not the best?

TWO

Farm

My life on the farm during the Great Depression more nearly resembled farm life of fully two thousand years ago than farm life today.

I have reflected on it often since that time; social eras change at their own curious pace, depending on geography and technology and a host of other factors. It is incredible with what speed these changes have totally transformed both the farming methods and the very lifestyle I knew in my boyhood.

We lived in a wooden clapboard house alongside the dirt road which led from Savannah to Columbus, Georgia, a house cool in the summer and cold in the winter. It was heated by fireplaces within two double chimneys, and by the wood stove in the kitchen. There was no source of heat in the northeast corner room where I slept, but hot bricks and a down comforter helped to ease the initial pain of a cold bed in winter.

For years we used an outdoor privy in the back yard for sanitation and a hand pump for water supply. Later, another shallow well was dug under our back porch and a hand pump was installed there, and eventually we had a windmill and running water in our home. In the bathroom was a cold shower and a commode and lavatory; it was not unusual during the winter to find the pipes frozen and the commode pushed off the wall and lying on the floor. Water for bathing had to be heated on the wood stove.

Our yards were covered with white sand, replenished every spring from a nearby sand pit. The yards were kept clean by sweeping once or twice a week with brush brooms and, typically, were occupied by dogs, chickens, guineas, ducks, and geese.

Fried chicken and chicken pie were often part of our regular meals, and there were hen nests located in every convenient place—alongside buildings, in the forks of trees, and wherever else the hens had an inclination to lay eggs. There was no fence around our yard, and we had frequent poultry fatalities on the road in front of our house. Guineas were especially vulnerable to the passing of cars.

The dominant feature of the backyard was the woodpile with large stocks of hickory and pine for burning in the fireplaces and the cooking stove. Pecan, mulberry, chinaberry, magnolia, and fig trees gave us shade and facilities for tree houses and climbing. All in all, it seemed a comfortable and enjoyable place to live.

Our lives then were centered almost completely around our own family and our own home.

I was an only son in those early years, my brother, Billy, not being born until I was thirteen years old, and my father was a very firm but understanding director of my life and habits. In retrospect, the farm work sounds primitive and burdensome, but at the time it was an accepted farm practice, and my dad himself was an unusually hard worker. Also, he was always my best friend.

My father, Earl, was an extremely competent farmer and businessman who later developed a wide range of interests in public affairs.

He was thirty years old when I was born, stood about five feet eight inches tall and weighed 175 pounds. He was a good athlete, played baseball as a pitcher on the local town team, and was an excellent tennis player. In fact, adjacent to our house, between the house and store, we had a tennis court on our farm. There were also three other tennis courts in Plains, and with the exception of high school baseball and basketball, tennis was our most important competitive sport while I was growing up. I could do well even against older high school boys, but I could never beat my father. He had a wicked sliced ball which barely bounced at all on the relatively soft dirt court.

Daddy loved to have a good time and enjoyed parties much

more than did my mother. I remember one occasion when my parents had a party at our home for doctor and nurse friends with whom my mother worked at a nearby hospital. Late at night, I became furious at the loud talking, laughing, and general merriment, and I got up from my bed, dressed, and went out into the yard with a blanket to sleep in my treehouse. After a few hours, the guests had all departed, and my father came out into the yard and called for me to come in. But I chose not to answer. The next morning I received one of the few whippings of my boyhood, all of which I remember so well.

One of the rare times I ever felt desperately sorry for my father was when he went to my uncle's general store to be measured by a traveling salesman for a tailor-made suit of clothes, the first of his life. Ordinarily all our clothes were ready made, so we waited with a keen anticipation for Daddy's new suit to arrive, and after it did, on the next Sunday morning when we began to dress for Sunday school and church, Daddy opened the box with a great flourish. All the family entered the bedroom, gathered around the fireplace while Daddy began to put on his suit.

Alas, some terrible mistake had been made! The custom-made clothes were twice as large as my father. I remember that no one in the family laughed.

My father was a natural leader in our community, and with the advent of the Rural Electrification Program, when I was about thirteen years old, my father became one of the first directors of our local REA organization. He then began to learn the importance of political involvement on a state and national basis to protect the program that meant so much in changing our farm lifestyle. He served for many years as a member of the county school board, and one year before his death in 1953, he was elected to the state legislature.

An almost unbelievable change took place in our lives when electricity came to the farm.

The continuing burden of pumping water, sawing wood, building fires in the cooking stove, filling lamps with kerosene, and closing the day's activity with the coming of night . . . all these things changed dramatically. Farmers began to have county and regional meetings to discuss the changes that were taking place in their lives, to elect REA directors, to discuss national legislation, to determine rate structures, to bargain with the Georgia Power Company on electricity supplies, and to determine which new areas would be covered next by the electric power line.

In general, our family's horizons were expanded greatly.

The new availability of electricity was a great relief to me in a curiously personal way.

Electric mule clippers took the place of the handcranked machine which Daddy had always used to shear the mules and to cut my hair. On one early occasion, I was planning to go to Columbus to visit my mother's parents, and I was very nervous about the long trip. In preparation for the trip my father took me into the backyard to cut my hair. The clippers were driven by a flexible steel cable which another person turned by a hand crank. Daddy's hand slipped, and a big gap was cut out of the hair on top of my head. After studying the situation for a few minutes, he decided that the only solution was to clip my head completely so at least it would be uniform, and this he did.

I was deeply embarrassed and wanted to stay at home until my

The Carter home from 1928 to 1949, photo taken in 1948

*Earl Carter, Jimmy's
father, while in the
service during the
First World War*

hair grew out. Finally, Daddy found a cap that I could wear, and I
went to Columbus to visit for about a week and then returned
home. Later, my mother asked my grandmother what she thought
of me, and Grandma reported that I was a fine boy but acted in a
very peculiar way. She told Mother I was the only child she had
ever seen who slept and ate while wearing a cap!

One reason I never thought about complaining about the work
assigned to me as a boy was that my father always worked harder
than did I or anyone else on the farm. In nearby Plains, Daddy
opened a small office where he bought peanuts from other farmers
on a contract basis for a nearby oil mill, and where he eventually
began to sell fertilizer, seed, and other supplies to neighboring
farmers.

I never even considered disobeying my father, and he seldom,
if ever, ordered me to perform a task; he simply suggested that it

needed to be done, and he expected me to do it. But he was a stern disciplinarian and punished me severely when I misbehaved. From the time I was four years old until I was fifteen years old he whipped me six times, and I've never forgotten any of those impressive experiences. The punishment was administered with a small, long, flexible peach-tree switch.

My most vivid memory of a whipping was when I was four or five years old. I had been to my Sunday school class, and as was his custom, Daddy had given me a penny for the offering. When we got back home, I took off my Sunday clothes and put the contents of my pocket on a dresser. There were two pennies lying there. Daddy thus discovered that when they passed the collection plate I had taken out an extra penny, instead of putting mine in for the offering. That was the last money I ever stole.

Most of my other punishments occurred because of arguments with my sister Gloria, who was younger than I but larger during our growing years. I remember once she threw a wrench and hit me, and I retaliated by shooting her in the rear end with a BB gun. For several hours, she re-burst into tears every time the sound of a car was heard. When Daddy finally drove into our yard, she was apparently sobbing uncontrollably, and after a brief explanation by her of what had occurred, Daddy whipped me without further comment.

I never remember seeing Daddy without a hat on when he was outdoors. He laughed a lot and almost everybody liked him. He kept very thorough and accurate farm and business records and was scrupulously fair with all those who dealt with him. He finished the tenth grade at Riverside Academy in Gainesville, Georgia, before the First World War. So far as I have been able to determine this was—at that time—the most advanced education of any Carter man since our family moved to Georgia more than two hundred years ago.

My father died in July of 1953, a victim of cancer. He was extremely intelligent, well read about current events, and was always probing for innovative business techniques or enterprises. He was quite conservative, and my mother was and is a liberal, but within our family we never thought about trying to define such labels.

Jimmy at age five and his sister Gloria at age three

My mother is a registered nurse, and during my formative years she worked constantly, primarily on private duty either at the nearby hospital or in patients' homes. She typically worked on nursing duty twelve hours per day or twenty hours per day, for which she was paid a magnificent six dollars, and during her off-duty hours she had to perform the normal functions of a mother and a housekeeper. She served as a community doctor for our neighbors and for us and was extremely compassionate towards all those who were afflicted with any sort of illness. Although my father seldom read a book, my mother was an avid reader, and so was I.

Quite often my mother was not paid for her nursing service at all, at least not in cash. I remember that once for weeks Mother nursed a young girl who had diphtheria. The girl's parents were very poor. Eventually she died, and a few weeks later the girl's father drove into our yard with a one-horse wagon loaded down with turpentine chips. He had traveled more than a day to get there.

Although the wood chips had little monetary value, they were extremely helpful to us because they burst instantly into a roaring flame when touched with a match and were useful in starting a fire in the stove or fireplace, an early morning necessity for us. I remember that we unloaded the turpentine chips into a pit used for storing ferns and flowers during the winter, and we benefitted from their use for several years.

My mother's youngest sister, "Sissy," was very close to us, and when she was married, we had the wedding dinner at our home. The whole family worked for days preparing a delicious meal to impress our many visitors who came there from throughout the state of Georgia. The main course was chicken salad. In the midst of the meal, as our guests sat under the shade trees in our yard in their fancy clothes, dozens of chickens began to die before our eyes.

We scrambled wildly to pick up the dead chickens before our guests could see them. No one died of ptomaine poisoning, and we discovered later that those chickens in our yard had eaten poisonous nitrate of soda which had been left in open bags in the field adjoining our house.

My black playmates were the ones who joined me in field work that was suitable for younger boys. We were the ones who "toted" fresh water to the more adult workers in the field. We mopped the cotton, turned sweet potato and watermelon vines, pruned the deformed young watermelons, toted the stove wood, swept the yards, carried slop to the hogs, and gathered eggs—all thankless tasks. But we also rode mules and horses through the woods, jumped out of the barn loft into huge piles of oat straw, wrestled and fought, fished and swam. Their mothers had complete authority over me when I was in their homes (I don't remember that their fathers did). My best and closest friend while growing up was named A. D. Davis. He now works for a sawmill and has, I believe, fourteen children.

During high-school years we had at Archery a baseball team consisting of ten players. (The tenth player was the "back stop" who stood behind the catcher to block balls which escaped.)

The nearby town of Plains had a population of about 550, and was for me a center of commerce, education, and religion. A small cotton gin was located there, and there was a market for peanuts, watermelons, eggs, cantaloupe, cream, butter, blackberries, and other farm products.

Our school was located in Plains, where I completed eleven years, in those days a total high school education, before going off to college; and each Sunday we attended the Plains Baptist Church, where my father was a Sunday school teacher.

During my childhood I never considered myself a part of the Plains society, but always thought of myself as a visitor when I entered that "metropolitan" community.

In my class in the Plains school we had about thirty students when we started, and eleven years later our graduating class consisted of twenty-four members. Total membership in the Plains Baptist Church was about 300, but we ordinarily had and still have about 150 at Sunday school for each service. It is by far the biggest church in town.

My father had a little store next to our home where we sold overalls, work shoes, sugar, salt, flour, meal, coffee, Octagon Soap, tobacco and snuff, rat traps, castor oil, lamp wicks, and kerosene.

Plains, Georgia, in 1925. It remains much the same today. The store at the extreme left was operated by Earl Carter until 1928.

Our own farm products were kept in stock, such as syrup, side meat, lard, cured hams, loops of stuffed sausage, and wool blankets. The store was open on Saturdays during payday and otherwise was unlocked only when a customer came, almost always during meal times, for a nickel's worth of snuff or kerosene.

During the field-work season all the workers arose each morning at 4 A.M., sun time, wakened by the ringing of a large farm bell. We would go to the barn and catch the mules by lantern light, put the plow stocks, seed, fertilizer, and other supplies on the wagons, and drive to the field where we would be working that day. Then we would unhook the mules from the wagon harness, hook up the plows, and wait for it to be light enough to cultivate without plowing up the crops.

When I was a small boy, I carried water from a nearby spring in buckets to the men, and filled up the seed planters and fertilizer distributors, or ran errands. Later, I was proud to plow by myself.

We worked steadily with brief breaks to let the mules rest, or for breakfast and dinner, and then at sundown we would hook the mules to the wagons and go back to the barn lot. There was no running water there, so we then fed and pumped water for the livestock and went home for supper and to an early bed.

On other days we moved slowly up and down the field, hoeing weeds and grass. There was always a lot of conversation, and at times the whole group sang together to provide a rhythmical beat for the chopping of the hoes.

Our blacksmith shop was a small building near the barn with, of course, a dirt floor. The forge and anvil, drill press, and emery wheel were used daily to repair farm tools and sometimes to make them. Our horses and mules were shod there, and our plow points were sharpened.

A few of us did this work routinely, but Daddy handled the more difficult jobs. The rudiments of blacksmithing were a required part of our Future Farmers of America training at school; and the shop was always filled with and surrounded by every imaginable kind of scrap-iron.

We learned to appreciate the stability of the agricultural programs brought about by federal government action, and we cooperated fully in the soil and water conservation service plans for erosion control and the enhancement of wildlife. But my father never forgave President Franklin Roosevelt for requiring that hogs be slaughtered and cotton be plowed up when these production control programs first went into effect. He never again voted for Roosevelt.

Wages paid on the farm were very low. I remember when they increased from $1.00 *per day* up to $1.25 for adult men. Women were paid $.75 and children $.25 for a day's work in the field. Yet no rent was charged for farm houses, and garden patches and free wood to be cut in the forests helped make ends meet. In almost every family someone trapped, hunted, or fished. White corn was milled into meal and grits, and wheat into flour. Soap and lard were made on the farm. Most repairs could be made with hay wire, which was everywhere. Supplies and clothing, at least in earned wages, were still expensive. A pair of overalls cost $1.00, and a pair of work shoes, $1.50.

Since we had no refrigeration except small wooden iceboxes served by the semi-weekly traveling ice man, we cooperated for a few months each year with our neighbors in assuring a steady supply of beef. Eight farmers usually comprised a beef club, and every two weeks or so we would gather on a Saturday morning at one of the member's homes to slaughter and dress a calf of a predetermined size. A rotating formula was devised to assure that throughout the eight-phased cycle each participant would receive the same quality cuts of meats. On rare occasions lamb would be eaten, and sometimes goats would be barbecued, but our primary sources of meat were poultry and beef, plus a lot of pork, both fresh and cured.

We measured time primarily by the seasons, with our habits and attitudes modified considerably by the farm chores and the ripening fruits and vegetables associated with the changing times of year.

There was work enough to be done by the men when it rained, but as young boys, my playmates and I tended to live in the woods and swamps. We fished in the creeks with set hooks when the water was rising following a rain, primarily fishing for catfish and freshwater eels. When the high water receded, we fished in water holes in the swamp by "mudding," stirring the mud up in the bottom of the hole with a hoe or with our feet until the fish would come up to the top for oxygen and we could scoop them up with our hands or a homemade net.

One of the exciting times of the year was when the redhorse suckers were running. Then the men and boys would descend on the small creeks, stand in the swift cold water at night with a flashlight, and gig the suckers as they swam upstream on their annual pilgrimage. The suckers were fearsome fighters, and the meat was delicious if slashed in thin strips so that the tiny bones could be thoroughly cooked. Although there are still these fish, suckers, in the large creeks, the many dams on our main rivers now make this ocean-to-headwater annual pilgrimage impossible.

I was an excellent tree climber, and the raccoon and possum hunters invited me frequently to go with them at night to climb up and shake down the treed animals. I remember once that the dogs treed just over a small moonshine still, much to the embarrassment of the hunter whose home was only a couple of hundred yards away.

We had dogs as our own constant companions, used for playmates and also for hunting squirrels, rabbits, coons, possums, and other similar small game. My father always had several good quail dogs on the farm, but I used these only after I was about ten years old.

Our farm work was heavy all year round. My daddy saw to that with his widely diversified farm industries. My schoolwork always came first, but farm children could expect the teachers to give few time-consuming homework assignments. There was always a yard to sweep, stove wood to cut and stack, water to pump, eggs to gather, chickens to feed, and the store to tend. These were all routine yard jobs and not related to the larger farm effort or to any seasonal changes.

Beginning immediately after Christmas we began the slow and tedious task of breaking all the cultivatable land with two-horse turning plows, going around and around the field until we finally wound up in the middle. On rare occasions during the new year,

Young Jimmy

we had to complete harvesting a small portion of our peanut crops or scrap the remaining stalks of cotton from the fields, but this was only if we had not experienced good harvest weather during the fall.

Before land where cotton had been planted could be turned, the heavy stalks had to be chopped, usually with a wide, heavy, mule-drawn roller with sharp blades mounted crosswise, which was pulled down the cotton row. Later, the land was harrowed with discs and dragged with a spike-tooth harrow or rakes to pile up the Bermuda grass for burning in the field. Bermuda grass was a constant and almost uncontrollable plague for us then. Sometimes it won the battle, and part of a field would be abandoned and no longer be cultivated.

On most occasions, after the land was ultimately smooth, the rows would be bedded up with turning plows. As the planting season approached, mule-drawn guano distributors would run down the center of the row bed, and later the seeds would be planted a few inches to the side or above the placement of the fertilizer itself.

The first planting of corn began as early as March, followed by cotton, then peanuts and other crops. During my boyhood the shift had been made from a dependence on cotton towards peanuts as a primary crop. Cultivation was begun almost as soon as the seed sprouted, or in the case of peanuts, even before the new plants were visible, by dragging harrows across the fields to kill the more rapidly emerging grass.

Peanuts are our most important crop in the Plains community, and there has never been any close competitor in my lifetime. Roughly twelve thousand tons of peanuts are marketed here each season. Georgia, by the way, produces about 40 percent of the nation's total peanuts—more than any other two states combined.

Boiled peanuts, incidentally, should be considered one of the great gifts of God to mankind—but only when done in proper fashion. Let me explain what I mean. Peanuts grow under the ground like potatoes. This is a unique plant which blooms above ground, then sends a tiny pointed tendril about the size of a toothpick down to pierce the surface of the earth, and after it is about two inches deep the end of the pointed "pin" swells up to make

*Cousin Hugh Carter
with baby Jimmy*

the nut. When planted reasonably close together each vine produces about fifty nuts. If the peanuts are picked off the vines immediately after they leave the ground they contain about 35 percent
moisture. If boiled in very salty water until done, they are delicious.

From the time I was five years old I sold boiled peanuts on the
streets of Plains. After I reached high school age, each Saturday I
joined with my cousin, Hugh Carter, in the sale of five-cent ham-
burgers and homemade ice cream, three dips for a nickel. (Years
later Hugh was elected to the state senate seat which I gave up to
run for governor.)

Every afternoon I would go out into my daddy's field during the proper season, pull peanuts up out of the ground, stack them on a small wagon, and pull them back to our yard. After pulling the nuts from the green vines, I would pump water and wash them carefully to remove the dirt from the hulls. After soaking overnight, the peanuts were boiled early the next morning in salt water, and approximately one-half pound would be put into each of about twenty paper bags. Then I would walk the two or three miles down the railroad tracks to Plains to sell my boiled peanuts on the streets. When they were all sold, I came back home to repeat the process.

Even at that early age of not more than six years, I was able to distinguish very clearly between the good people and the bad people of Plains. The good people, I thought, were the ones who bought boiled peanuts from me! I have spent much time since then in trying to develop my ability to judge other people, but that was the simplest method I ever knew, despite its limitations. I think about this every time I am tempted to judge other people hastily.

Quite often, there were interesting events in Plains to divert me from my peanut salesmanship. Medicine shows visited there every few months. There were log-cutting contests conducted by ax salesmen. A tiny circus would come once a year, and the local community conducted such affairs as Hallowe'en carnivals. Also, there was always a marble game, top spinning, or checkers to be played, and on good sales days I participated in these contests after all my peanuts were sold.

I got to be a businessman in those days, on a small scale, even if it seemed on a big scale for me. I would earn about $1.00 per day gross income selling peanuts, and on Saturdays sometimes I could sell as much as five times that amount. By the time I was nine years old I had saved enough money to purchase five bales of cotton at the then all-time low price of $.05 per pound. I kept this cotton in one of my daddy's farm storehouses until the price increased after a few years to $.18, at which time I sold it for enough money to purchase five houses, owned at the time by the estate of the recently deceased local undertaker. From then until I left home to enter the Naval Academy, I collected $16.50 in rent each month from those five houses. Two rented for $5.00 each, two for $2.00 each, and one for $2.50. The houses were finally sold to the tenants in 1949 while I was living in Hawaii as a naval officer.

Sometimes I felt lonesome and timid as a small salesman. It wasn't always easy to sell those twenty bags of boiled peanuts each day. I had about ten regular customers, including our cobbler who always bought two bags. The others had to be sold to checker players around the service stations, the mule stable, or the garage, or to customers who visited Plains to shop.

One of the few unpleasant experiences I remember was when a wise guy at the local garage offered to buy a bag of peanuts if I could obey some hand signals that he would give me. I was only seven or eight years old. The checker players and other loafers watched while I moved back and forth and from side to side with my eyes fixed on the movement of the man's hands, until he finally guided me to step on a lighted cigarette with my bare feet. A few of the onlookers laughed, while I tried not to cry.

In those days, the most fearful prospect was continued rains, because many crops could be lost to the dominant weeds and grass. I remember my father often walking back and forth in the yard looking up at the sky, praying that the weather would be clear enough to plow the crop before it rained again. Nowadays the weeds and grass are controlled primarily by herbicides, and crop yields can be increased considerably by heavier continuing rains; drought is today the most fearful weather prospect.

Primary crops of cotton, corn, and peanuts were planted with mule-drawn equipment. Other major crops were planted by hand, such as sweet potatoes, Irish potatoes, and watermelons. During rainy days, too, there was plenty of work to be done in the fields. Sweet potato vines and watermelon vines had to be turned from one furrow middle to the other to permit plowing without destroying the long vines. Cotton had to be mopped with poison. Nitrate of soda fertilizer was applied by hand in small quantities adjacent to each individual stalk of corn or cotton during the growing season.

But the constant pressure was controlling grass by plowing, and cultivating with the mules would be continued until the crops became too large to plow. The cotton limbs would meet in the middle and would be broken as the cultivating equipment went through. We would still be plowing corn when it was higher than a mule's ear, and at the end of each row we would have to stop and untangle the thousands of corn roots from around our plow foot.

We did not realize that we were cutting yield so drastically until more recent times when we learned how much damage cultivation can do to a crop while it is actually growing or putting on fruit.

At the conclusion of the growing season, usually early in June, came "lay-by" time when we no longer had to plow the growing crops. Grain was then cut and shocked, and it was hauled to a stationary machine and thrashed when dry. Watermelons were cut and hauled to town, packed in railroad cars and shipped to Northern markets. This went on each season until the freight bill equalled the declining value of the shipped melons. But these chores were enjoyable compared to the constant plowing and hoeing which had earlier pressed heavily on everyone.

After these few weeks of relatively easy work, the harvest season came for the major crops: cotton had to be picked by hand; peanuts were pulled out of the ground, the dirt shaken off them, and then stacked on poles to dry. Later, the corn leaves were pulled and the fodder tied in little bundles and stuck on top of the corn stalk to dry. Velvet beans, which were often planted in the same rows with corn, were picked, and the stinging fuzz made this one of the most difficult of all farm jobs. Still later, we pulled the corn ears by hand and piled them in the field to be picked up in wagons and hauled to the barn. We thrashed peanuts by hauling the dried stacks on wagons or sleds to a stationary peanut picker where the vines were separated from the nuts. The peanut hay was baled for livestock feed, and the nuts were hauled to market.

These chores carried us into wintertime when hogs were slaughtered and meat cured. Sugar cane was cut in the fields, ground into juice, and the juice boiled into syrup. Oak and hickory wood were cut into logs, and the logs stacked into cords for use in fireplaces during the winter. Pine was split for stove wood.

Then, the annual cycle would repeat itself. And throughout

the whole year there were constant repetitive chores such as caring for the livestock, pumping water, milking cows, shearing sheep, and other similar jobs that required daily attention.

Some of these jobs were enjoyable; some were pure drudgery. But there was always an ability to look back and see specifically what had been accomplished during the day's work. We always took advantage of opportunities to explore the woods, fields, and swamps, to fish and hunt, to harvest fruits and vegetables from the garden and orchards, and to harvest wild fruits and nuts during their seasons.

The combined work and play of this early farm life gave me rich, varied experiences.

We enjoyed a highly diverse farm industry producing watermelons, peanuts, cotton, sweet potatoes, sugar cane syrup, honey, wool, goose feathers, milk, meat from hogs and cattle, blackberries, fruits and vegetables, timber products, and processed items from these raw materials.

My father was very aggressive and innovative in selling to other stores, and through his own country store, items produced and manufactured on the farm itself. For instance, wool from our sheep was sent off and exchanged for finished blankets; down pillows, featherbeds, and comforters from the goose down—which we picked every six months from the breasts of our flock—were kept for ourselves or sold just to "special" people; and syrup with a brand name of "Plains Maid" was a recognized product in all the surrounding country stores.

When Daddy first started selling Plains Maid syrup, we made it in an open, bowl-shaped kettle about eight feet in diameter and would simply grind the cane stalks with a mule-drawn roller press, tote the juice in buckets to the kettle where an oak log fire was burning under it, and keep cooking until it was the right consistency for syrup, constantly skimming off the frothy wastes which bubbled to the top.

In later years, my father bought a steam-driven mill for grinding the cane stalks and for heating an inclined pan. The juice was piped continuously to the top of the pan and would run slowly back and forth between baffles from one side to the other, being boiled by heat from the steam plant. The inclination of the pan would determine how fast the juice ran down and, therefore, how long it was boiled, and the juice was changed into syrup before it reached the bottom of the twenty-foot-long slanted pan. The thickness of the syrup was measured by a hydrometer, and the pan was tilted slightly up and down to control the consistency of the syrup. Some of the workers at the cane mill would secretly drink the "cane buck," which was fermented skimmings and made a very powerful alcoholic beverage.

My father also separated sweet milk into its component parts, and we sold cream and butter to the grocery stores and peddled chocolate milk in five-cent bottles to stores and filling stations. During the winter we would slaughter twenty to forty hogs at a time on a cold day and process all the meat, curing hams, grinding sausage, rendering lard, making souse meat, pickling pigs' feet, and so forth. Wild cherries, peaches, blackberries, and muscadines were made into jelly and jam and sometimes into wine for my parents' and their friends' consumption. And some of our vegetables were processed into finished products, such as catsup made from homegrown tomatoes during season.

One of the most distasteful jobs on the farm was mopping cotton. With the advent of boll weevils during the 1920s, it was necessary to poison cotton buds to control the insects. The normal process used was to mix arsenic, molasses, and water, to pour this conglomeration into a bucket, and to walk down each row of cotton with a rag mop on the end of a stick, dip the mop into the bucket, and apply a small quantity of the mixture into the bud of each cotton plant. It was a job for boys and not men, and we despised this task. After a few hours in the field our trousers, legs, and bare feet would become saturated with the syrupy mess. The flies would swarm around us and at night when we took off our trousers we had to stand them in the corner because the legs would not bend.

We enjoyed most of the farm work, however. Hauling cotton to the gin or watermelons to the railroad siding was always an exciting experience. Work in the blacksmith shop was also an interesting challenge.

We raised most of our food, and sweet potatoes were a major

part of my diet on the farm. In the fall when harvested, they were stored for the winter in "potato hills." A layer of potatoes was placed on straw and covered up again with another layer of straw, then a layer of dirt, then another layer of potatoes embedded on top and bottom by straw, then another layer of dirt. The hill was shaped like a cone, and on the outside, dirt was packed six inches to a foot thick. All of this was to prevent the potatoes from being frostbitten. Every few days during the winter we would dig some of them out of the hill and keep them in the house for cooking. We children often cooked our own by burying them in the hot ashes in the living room fireplace. Irish potatoes were stored in a dry place—either under the house or in an attic. Fruits like peaches and apples were sliced and dried on tin roofs in the summer sun, then stored in loose cotton bags in the house during the winter. Most other vegetables, fruits, and jellies were canned. Meat was cured using salt and spices and hung in the smokehouse. Daddy experimented by burning different kinds of wood to change the flavor of the meat-curing smoke.

During the Depression years, which happened to be the time I was growing up on the farm, the amount of labor expended compared to any sort of cash return was almost unbelievable. In the depths of the Depression, peanuts sold for as little as one cent per pound. It was "hard times," incredibly so. A farmer with his own manual labor and using a mule and mule-drawn equipment would break an acre of land, harrow at least twice, lay off rows, apply fertilizer, plant the seed, cultivate seven or eight times, plow up the peanuts, shake each vine manually and then place on a stack pole, let them cure for eight to ten weeks, haul the stack poles to the threshing machine, separate the peanuts from the vine, and carry his entire crop to market.

After all that, the average yield that low year was seven hundred pounds per acre, which gave him a *gross* return for all his year's work on that acre of only seven dollars! The average farmer planted about fifteen acres of this primary crop.

Deer are plentiful in Georgia today, but there were very few during my boyhood days. I can remember seeing only two of them during all those early years in the woods. Turkeys were more plentiful.

There were always weekly hunts during dove season. In those

days we were permitted by law to shoot doves all during the day. The normal custom was to assemble in a farmer's home or in one of the stores downtown a couple of hours before daybreak. Some of the men would have a few drinks, others would drink black coffee, and then we would proceed to the field while it was still dark. Everyone had a shell box and lightwood available to make a fire in the freezing weather. When daylight began to break, the doves would come into the field and firing would start. For several years I picked up doves for my father before I myself was permitted to shoot. Around nine or ten o'clock in the morning, my father would carry me by the schoolhouse, and with a big smile I would enter the classroom, covered with bird feathers.

Within my memory, whenever anyone has ever asked me what I wanted for Christmas or my birthday present, I always replied, "Books." When I was four years old my godmother, also a nurse like my mother—though apparently not a great reader—gave me a set of the complete works of Guy de Maupassant. It was, of course, years later before I read through this set of volumes.

My life was heavily influenced by our school superintendent, Miss Julia Coleman, who encouraged me to learn about music, art, and especially literature.

Miss Julia was a spinster, who died recently, and she encouraged all of her students to seek cultural knowledge beyond the requirements of a normal rural school classroom. We were highly competitive in debating, an essay contest called "Ready Writing," music appreciation, one-act play productions, spelling bees, and other cultural activities.

Every student in the classroom was required to debate, to memorize and recite long poems and chapters from the Bible, and to participate in spelling contests. Each of us had to learn the rudiments of music and play some musical instrument—if it were only a ukulele, harmonica, or even a small piccolo.

Miss Julia had poor eyesight, and the discipline of her classrooms evaporated during her later years of supervising schoolwork. However, this was certainly not the case when I was her student.

As a schoolboy who lived in an isolated farm community, my exposure to classical literature, art, and music was insured by this superlative teacher. She prescribed my reading list and gave me a silver star for every five books read and a gold star for ten book reports.

Miss Julia remains alive in my memory. She was short and somewhat crippled, yet she was quite graceful as she moved along. Her face was expressive, particularly when she was reading one of the poems she loved, or presenting to a class the paintings of Millet, Gainesborough, Whistler, or Sir Joshua Reynolds.

When I was about twelve years old she called me in and stated that she was ready for me to read *War and Peace*. I was happy with the title because I thought that finally Miss Julia had chosen for me a book about cowboys and Indians. I was appalled when I checked the book out of the library because it was about fourteen hundred pages long, written by the Russian novelist Tolstoy, and of course not about cowboys at all. It turned out to be one of my favorite books, and I have read it two or three times since then. The book is about the French army under Napoleon, who believed that he was destined to be the conqueror of the world. He attacked Russia with every expectation of an early victory, but he under-estimated the severity of the Russian winter and the love of the peasants for their land. The following spring the French army withdrew in defeat.

War and Peace is a great book about one of the most important events in modern history. This was the crucial campaign of Napoleon, who led the greatest army ever assembled until then— with fighting men from twenty nations.

The course of history was changed as great men struggled for military and political power. But the book is not written about the Emperor or the Czar. It is mostly about the students, farmers, bar-bers, housewives, and common soldiers.

As stated by Tolstoy, the purpose of the book is to show that the course of human events—even the greatest historical events— is determined ultimately not by the leaders, but by the common, ordinary people. Their hopes and dreams, their doubts and fears, their courage and tenacity, their quiet commitments determine the destiny of the world.

If the author were correct in his claim that the destiny of

nations is controlled by the people, even when they are ruled despotically by kings and emperors, how much more true should this be in a nation like ours where each of us is free! Our government is supposed to be shaped and controlled by the collective wisdom and judgment of those among us who are willing to exert this power and democratic authority. But often those who want no special favors from government do not participate actively in the political process.

In general, the early years of my life on the farm were full and enjoyable, isolated but not lonely. We always had enough to eat, no economic hardship, but no money to waste. We felt close to nature, close to the members of our family, and close to God.

THREE

Archery

Our farm was at Archery, about three miles west of Plains, Georgia. Archery was not incorporated or organized in any way; it was only the name of the rural community and train stop. Our farm and store were about one-half mile east of Archery on the dirt road towards Plains.

Plains was a town, then and now, of about 550 people. In the undefined community of Archery there lived two permanent families who were white, one my own family and the other that of the Seaboard Railroad section foreman. There were usually one or two more transient white families and about twenty-five black families in the community.

In those days, Archery society was built around a black leader who was Bishop of the African Methodist Episcopal Church for five or six states. His name was Bishop William Johnson, and he was undoubtedly the most prestigious person in the community. He had founded a small school and operated an insurance company based on a fraternal order.

Each year the Bishop would invite us—the nearby white people —to special worship services at the Archery AME Church, and a superb choir would come down from Morris Brown College in Atlanta to take part in the program.

One of the Johnson sons lived and was educated in the North, in Boston, I believe. His name was Alvan, and he became a very good friend of us children and my mother. He was the only black man who habitually came to our front door. Whenever we heard

that Alvan was back home for a visit, there was a slight nervous-
ness around our house. We would wait in some combination of
anticipation and trepidation until we finally heard the knock on
our front door.

My daddy would leave and pretend it wasn't happening while
my mother received Alvan in the front living room to discuss his
educational progress and his experiences in New England. For this
was one of the accepted proprieties of the segregated South which
Alvan violated. Even when Bishop Johnson came to see my father,
he would park in front of the store and send one of his drivers to
the back door to inform my daddy that he would like to see him,
and Daddy would go out to meet the Bishop in the yard.

We did have one of the first diesel locomotives in the area.
The entire train consisted of three cars (the whole train did) and
carried the mail from Columbus, Georgia, at the Alabama-Georgia
line, to the east. It contained one passenger car which made a
round trip each day. Anyone in the rural area around Archery who
wanted to ride the train had to walk up the track about a quarter
mile and stick up a little red leather flag in the end of a cross tie.
The engineer would see the flag and stop at the railroad crossing.

I guess because the train's horn sounded like a cow bleating in
agony, or perhaps because of that diesel's configuration in contrast
to the normal steam locomotives of the time, everyone called it
"The Butt Head." It cost fifteen cents to travel to Americus about
thirteen miles away.

I am the oldest of four children. My sister Gloria is two years
younger than I, and my sister Ruth came three years later, followed
after eight years by my brother, Billy.

In the family of Mr. Watson, the railroad section foreman,
there were two boys and two girls, all of them older than I. The
two boys were superb athletes, and the young one later played
semipro basketball. The oldest one, named Bernece, died at the
age of about twenty when our local doctor treated him for consti-
pation, not realizing that his appendix had ruptured.

Before we had any school buses, we would sometimes catch a
ride to the schoolhouse in Plains in the Watsons' car. Our very first
school bus was a homemade contrivance mounted on an old, bent,

pickup-truck chassis. It would seat about fifteen students on the two benches, and the body of the bus was absurdly mounted at about a ten degree angle to the direction of movement. The other kids who rode in regular school buses called ours a "cracker box." Those first school buses were for white children only, as in that time there were dozens of small schools located all over the county within walking distance of the black children's homes.

One of the proud moments of my life came when I was given a white canvas belt and a tin badge and sworn in as a School Boy Patrolman. My job was to enforce all the safety precautions but, also, to go to the nearest house for help when our makeshift bus frequently slid into a ditch during rainy weather.

The center of the Archery community was the train stop, the AME Church, Bishop Johnson's school, the railroad section houses, and a tiny store—across the road from the church—which was covered completely on the roof and sides with straightened-out Prince Albert Tobacco cans. The Archery school was a large, two-story frame building with living quarters, office, and classrooms.

The most important event which ever occurred in Archery was the funeral of Bishop Johnson. Preachers and choirs came from everywhere, and the whole settlement was amazed at the stream of big black Cadillacs, Packards, and Lincolns which had come from other states. Dozens of his white friends from the surrounding communities attended the services. Bishop Johnson died in 1936 when I was twelve years old.

The hot southern sun was a gift in my childhood. Between early April and the end of October we never wore shoes, and seldom wore a shirt except for church or school.

Our toys were found or made on the farm. We rolled steel barrel hoops with a heavy wire pusher, slid down pine-straw hills on old disc plow blades, hunted with slingshots and flips, flew homemade kites and June bugs on a string, and threw spinning projectiles made of corn cobs and chicken feathers. We dug honey out of bee trees and harvested wild plums, blackberries, persimmons, chufas, and sassafras roots. We built dams on the small streams, and treehouses where we lived overnight or for weekends. We hunted arrowheads in the fields.

Every now and then one of my schoolmates from Plains would stay with me overnight, and for a long time I had a close friend named Rembert Forrest, whose family lived about five miles north of Archery. We would visit each other for as much as two weeks at a time, traveling between our homes on horseback or on foot through the Choctawhatchee Swamp. But with these exceptions and during brief periods of time when white families moved in and out of the neighborhood, all my playmates were black.

We hunted, fished, explored, worked, and slept together. We ground sugar cane, plowed with mules, pruned watermelons, dug and bedded sweet potatoes, mopped cotton, stacked peanuts, cut stovewood, pumped water, fixed fences, fed chickens, picked velvet beans, and hauled cotton to the gin together.

In addition to the many chores, we also found time to spend the night on the banks of Choctawhatchee and Kinchafoonee creeks, catching and cooking catfish and eels when the water was rising from heavy rains.

Brother Billy, at left, and Jimmy

We ran, swam, rode horses, drove wagons, and floated on rafts together. We misbehaved together and shared the same punishments. We built and lived in the same treehouses and played cards and ate at the same table.

But we never went to the same church or school. Our social life and our church life were strictly separate. We did not sit together on the two-car diesel train that could be flagged down in Archery. There was a scrupulous compliance with these unwritten and unspoken rules. I never heard them questioned. *Not then.*

We did not have electricity as I was growing up, but Daddy owned a battery-operated radio. The only programs we heard after dark as a family were prize fights and political conventions. I stayed up alone sometimes, after everyone else was asleep, to listen to Glenn Miller while lying on the floor in front of the fireplace.

I remember that our battery radio went dead on the night of the Republican Convention of 1936, so we took the radio outside and hooked it to the car battery in the yard. We sat on the ground and listened while Alf Landon was being nominated. I was not quite twelve years old.

All of our black neighbors came to see Daddy when the second Joe Louis–Max Schmeling fight was to take place. There was intense interest, and they asked if they could listen to the fight. We propped the radio up in the open window of our house, and we and our visitors sat and stood under a large mulberry tree nearby.

There were heavy racial overtones encompassing the fight, with Joe Louis given a good chance to become the new black heavyweight champion of the world. He had lost in his first boxing encounter with Schmeling, but in this return match Louis almost killed his opponent in the first round. My father was deeply disappointed in the outcome.

There was no sound from anyone in the yard, except a polite, "Thank you, Mister Earl," offered to my father.

Then our several dozen visitors filed across the dirt road, across the railroad track, and quietly entered a house about a hundred yards away out in the field. At that point, pandemonium broke loose inside that house, as our black neighbors shouted and yelled in celebration of the Louis victory. But all the curious, accepted proprieties of a racially segregated society had been carefully observed.

The first racial argument took place in our home when I was on leave from my navy submarine in 1950. We had a popular black sailor in the crew, and I was describing to my father an incident which had occurred on a recent visit to Nassau. Our entire ship's force had accepted an invitation from the British officials to attend an "official" party. As we were preparing for the occasion, a last-minute message was brought to us that, in accordance with the island's custom, only white members of the crew could attend. Not a single one of the submariners on our ship chose to attend the party. There was simply no way that I could explain the reasons to my father.

After that, he and I agreed to avoid racial subjects on my rare and brief visits home.

I have reflected many times about growing up in what was, as one young, progressive, New South congressman described it, the "white man's South." Despite the black playmates of my youth, I can remember that I was literally a grown man before I was thrown into social situations in which I routinely met and talked with black men and women on an equal basis.

It is disconcerting to remember with what mistaken notions many of us clung for a long time to the rigid structure of segregation without realizing for a while what a blessing it would be when we passed on to a new and free relationship. But it is not easy to give up old habits, and it is especially difficult when they are ingrained in almost unquestioned tradition.

Our home was right across the road from the Seaboard Railroad track. Like all farm boys I always had a flip, or slingshot. They had stabilized the railroad bed with little white round rocks, which I used for ammunition. I would frequently go out to the railroad and gather the most perfectly shaped rocks of proper size. There were always a few in my pockets, and others cached away around the farm so they would be convenient if I ran out of my pocket supply.

One day I was leaving the track with my pockets and hands full of rocks, and my mother came out on the front porch and called me. She had in her hands a plate full of cookies which she had just baked for me. She asked, "Honey, would you like some cookies?" Really, nothing much happened, but I still remember it vividly. I stood there about fifteen or twenty seconds, in honest doubt about whether I should drop those worthless rocks and take the cookies which Mother offered me with a heart full of love.

It is hard to understand in retrospect why we were so reluctant to drop the rocks of past years. To think about going back to segregated schools and public places, or, as was the case in Georgia, to a county unit system which deliberately cheated for generations both black and white voters of our state, is almost inconceivable. To circumvent the one man–one vote principle would now be considered a terrible violation of the basic principles of justice and equity.

One of the first speeches I made in the Georgia Senate was to urge the abolition of the infamous "thirty questions" which had been so proudly evolved as a subterfuge to keep black citizens from voting. They had been kept with a great deal of smirking and pride for generations—questions that nobody could answer, but which were asked in some counties to every black citizen who had the temerity to approach a county registrar and say, "I want to vote."

The civil-rights workers of the 1950s and 1960s, who were despised by many because they shook up the social structure that ostensibly benefited white people, were hardly greeted with approbation and accolades by our great jurists, lawyers, and political leaders. Instead, they were greeted with intense opposition and even fear when they demanded simply that black citizens and white citizens be treated the same. Still, once these changes were made, simple but difficult changes, few would want to go back to those attitudes and commitments which hung like a millstone around our necks under the label of "separate but equal."

It is now obvious that neither half of that label was accurate. We were certainly not separate, and the opportunities were never equal. All of us were fearful and constrained .

In the South among black and white people, it is difficult to answer the question, "Who got the freedom?"

FOUR

Military

Military duty has occupied a large portion of my life.

Even before I started in the first grade of school, I had already decided that I wanted to go to the U.S. Naval Academy at Annapolis, and my father agreed completely with this decision. I don't exactly remember the origin of the idea, but I think it was twofold.

First, my mother's youngest brother was an enlisted man in the regular U.S. Navy. He was my distant hero, then serving in the Pacific fleet, a man thoughtful enough to send me at intervals small mementos of his visits to the foreign and exotic countries of the world. A letter or a photograph from my Uncle Tom Gordy was a memorable occasion in my young life.

Uncle Tom was lightweight fleet boxing champion around 1938, and we still have a famous (at least within the family) photograph of him standing proudly with boxing gloves, slightly in front of a group of other men whom he had beaten. Our first family involvement in the Second World War came because of him.

My Uncle Tom, a radioman, was stationed on the island of Guam as part of a small communications contingent when the Pacific war started. He was captured a few days after the attack on Pearl Harbor, when the Japanese invaded that outpost island. His wife, Dorothy, and their three children lived in San Francisco, and after Guam was captured they moved to Georgia to live with my grandmother and us at Archery.

After about two years we were all notified by the Red Cross

that Tom was dead, and a few months later his widow and the children moved back to San Francisco to live with her own family.

She remarried a year or so later, but then when the war was over, Uncle Tom was found alive in Japan, having been an isolated prisoner and a member of a train crew working on a Japanese railroad. He had been terribly ill and weighed less than one hundred pounds. He eventually recovered after a long illness, but he and Dorothy were never reconciled, in part perhaps because of interference from members of our family and especially the blame which Tom's sisters placed on Dorothy because she had remarried.

The second reason for my early desire to attend Annapolis was that my college education would be assured, no small consideration during those early Depression years when the chance of a family-financed college education seemed slight. My daddy's service in the army during World War I as a first lieutenant caused him to hold in high esteem the military training at the service academies and, because of my Uncle Tom's influence, the Naval Academy was my first choice.

Even as a grammar-school child, I read books about the navy and Annapolis. I wrote to ask for the entrance requirements, not revealing my age, and I almost memorized the little catalog when it came. Then I planned my studies and choice of library books accordingly. I had ridiculous and secret fears that I would not meet the requirements.

Some of the physical requirements listed in the catalog gave me deep concern. "Malocclusion of teeth" was my biggest theoretical problem. When I ate fruit, the knowledge that my teeth did not perfectly meet interfered with my enjoying the flavor. There was another requirement which caused me to worry, one called "retention of urine." I was always ashamed to ask whether that last clinging drop would block my entire naval career!

It has made me think about a well-known story of the nineteenth-century painter James McNeill Whistler, whose most famous painting is "Whistler's Mother." At West Point in his student days he eventually flunked out after failing chemistry and reportedly declared years later: "Had silicon been a gas, I would have been a major general."

In 1942 my appointment to Annapolis came from Congressman Stephen Pace, a man whom my father had supported every two years, both in hopes of obtaining my appointment to Annapolis and also because our congressman specialized in legislation concerning peanuts—our major crop. I finally received the appointment a year in advance for 1943, so one year was spent as a Naval ROTC student at Georgia Tech in Atlanta, taking courses recommended by the navy. Except for brief vacation visits, it was eleven years before I returned home, at the time of the death of my father.

At Annapolis my lifetime commitment carried me through the homesickness and hazing of my freshman (plebe) year. As a matter of fact, I refused to take the abuse seriously and treated it as a game. Some of it was rough, and I understand that most of the hazing I experienced is now prohibited. We never ate a peaceful meal. There were constant questions, research, songs, poems, reports on obscure athletic events, and recitations required of us. Poor table manners, any interesting facial expression, mistaken answers, or off-tune notes were reasons for instant punishment.

One of the most common punishments was called "shoving out," which meant you had to sit in a normal position without actually touching the chair. Deprivation of food on occasion seemed even worse. Gross manners resulted in the punishment of eating under the table. Some upperclassmen would require us to bend over and then hit us with brooms, heavy aluminum bread pans or—worst of all—the long-handled serving spoons. In addition we often had to run around the arduous military track or obstacle course in the dark before reveille.

These punishments for infractions of official or unofficial rules were frequent and were combined with legal punishment: extra marching, rowing of heavy boats, deprivation of liberty, and assignment of recorded demerits. These were all part of everyday life. There was no way to escape, not even for the best behaved of midshipmen. It was sometimes a brutal form of training and testing. If one ever showed any weakness, he was assaulted from all sides with punishment and harassment, and forced out of the academy.

Midshipman Jimmy
Carter at Annapolis

The academic requirements were stringent, but in my opinion not so difficult as at Georgia Tech. Class groups were small and every lesson period was competitive. No one could complete all of the class assignments, so there was a constant pressure for both speed and accuracy. Practical experience and book study were well coordinated in gunnery, seamanship, navigation, astronomy, engineering, and naval tactics.

Everyone was required to take exactly the same curriculum with the exception of a foreign language. I chose Spanish.

One of the most fearsome requirements was in after-dinner speaking. It was necessary to prepare a speech, ostensibly humorous, or at least entertaining. Then, some fifteen or twenty of us would assemble in a group in formal attire and try to eat a banquet meal, presided over by a senior officer. About a third of us would be called on at each session to make our prepared speeches. No one knew who would be introduced next. Speaking and listening were equally painful, and cold sweat was everywhere. We learned how to dance from professional instructors—without girls. Fox trot, waltz, samba, and rhumba were required subjects.

I also ran cross country and "military track" at Annapolis and played on the under-140-pound football team in the intercompany league. I weighed 121 pounds when I arrived at the Naval Academy and 135 pounds five years later when I reported on board my first submarine.

I spent a lot of my time at Annapolis trying to supplement the rigid engineering curriculum with private liberal arts studies. I was interested in literature, philosophy, theology, art, and music.

We were paid only $4 a month the first year, $7 per month the second year, and $11 a month as first classmen. My roommate and I spent most of our meager money on classical phonograph records. Other midshipmen would visit our room, and we would argue for hours about the relative quality of performance of orchestras and concert soloists. For some reason, each time we reached the final part of "Tristan and Isolde," a large group would quietly gather in the corridor to listen to Liebestod.

I became an expert on the recognition of the world's ships and planes during that time. It came about because every few weeks we would be assigned guard duty for a day and be excused from classes. We stood guard for four hours, then were off duty for eight hours, during which time we had a rare freedom within the Academy confines, and one extension of activity was to receive special instruction in aircraft and ship recognition at the naval airbase across the river.

Hundreds of silhouettes of allied and enemy planes and ships had to be memorized, so that at a glance their identity could be discerned. The images would be flashed on a screen for just a fraction of a second, and I worked hard at it until I had mastered them all.

A few of us also learned to fly the seaplanes on that naval base. I remember one type of seaplane was an OS2U two-seater scout plane. Another was the old, slow, reliable PBY whose long-range capabilities were used in World War II for lonely ocean patrols and to pick up pilots and others who needed rescue from the surface of the sea. I learned to land and take off on the water, to navigate and maneuver the old planes. This was under the close supervision of the regular pilots who were using this instructional time to fulfill their flying-hours requirement for drawing flight pay. It was a pleasant diversion from routine studies.

This was during World War II, and each summer we went on an extensive training cruise, mostly on old battleships. We were at war with Germany, and their submarines were a constant threat.

Our ports of call were in Jamaica, Trinidad, Puerto Rico, the Virgin Islands, and other Caribbean locations. We worked at learning everything from naval strategy to "holystoning" the wooden decks (rubbing a white brick back and forth on the deck to polish the wood). For cleaning and maintenance chores, the regular ship's crewmen gave the orders, and we carried them out. At times, we were rationed as little as one gallon of fresh water a day, and we used salt water for bathing and washing clothes.

Sleep was scarce, and we constantly yearned for it. We slept topside on the decks, and an instant after reveille sounded, the salt water hosers would begin to wash down the deck. We had to scramble wildly to keep ourselves and our blankets dry.

My first such cruise was on the USS *New York*, an ancient battleship which was propelled by enormous reciprocating engines. The engine rooms and boiler rooms were under pressure, and the heat and humidity were a debilitating physical burden. We carried out a normal combat mission, and the midshipmen on board were rotated every week or so from one duty station to another so we could learn as much about the ship as possible. However, our battle stations and cleaning stations remained the same throughout the cruise.

I manned a 40 mm anti-aircraft gun battery during the frequent alerts, and as one of my less romantic duties I was among those responsible for cleaning the "after head" or, in landlubber's language, the rest room located in the rear of the ship. The toilet facilities consisted of a long trough mounted on each of the two bulkheads or walls in the wedge-shaped compartment farthest aft in the ship. A stream of salt water flowed constantly down the bottom of the trough to flush the human wastes into the sea. During rough weather, the water and wastes were thrown onto the deck, drenching the floor and also those who at the time were using the toilet. This was not a favorite cleaning station.

After a few weeks of patrolling we detected a German submarine, and during the violent zigzagging and maneuvering to escape, one of the ship's four propellers was either hit by a torpedo or struck a coral reef and broke a blade.

Shortly thereafter, we were ordered back into port for repairs. The damage was not serious, but as we zigzagged across the sea, every turn of the bent propeller caused the ship to lurch.

My job on the trip back to the mainland was still to clean the after head. Every time the broken propeller would turn over, the rear end of the ship would jump just high enough to slosh the salt water onto the floor. In spite of heroic efforts, this cleaning situation deteriorated drastically. Our cleaning crew always thought there should have been a special service star to go on the combat ribbon the navy gave us.

We were required to wear kapok life jackets at all times, and each night we slept on them topside near our anti-aircraft gun stations. One of the disconcerting experiences of my life was when one of the other midshipmen inadvertently dropped into the ocean his flattened kapok life preserver, a filthy jacket that he had used as a mattress for several weeks. *It sank.*

The following year we were at sea in the North Atlantic when the atomic bombs were dropped on Hiroshima and Nagasaki. We had all been deeply concerned about the tremendous potential loss of life which would be required in the coming invasion of Japan. This was considered to be an inevitable action to end the war. The possible strategic and tactical decisions concerning the conclusion of the war were continuously debated. We would try to estimate how many hundreds of thousands of Americans and Japanese would be killed. No one ever thought the Japanese would surrender, so there seemed to be no alternative to a massive invasion.

When the announcement was made aboard ship that President Truman had a military message of great import for our nation, we thought immediately that perhaps the invasion had already begun. Hundreds of sailors sat on the steel decks in front of the ship's loudspeakers, and we listened to the flat voice of President Truman as he gave us the incomprehensible description of the new atomic weapon which had just been dropped on Japan. There was no way to understand the meaning of the nuclear weapons used in the attack on the two Japanese cities. We had never heard even a rumor of this quantum leap in destructive power.

After a few days the news of Japan's surrender came while we were still at sea. We were especially envious of those who were celebrating the victory in Times Square.

I certainly had no idea that my later naval career would be devoted to learning how to use atomic power for more peaceful purposes: for propelling ships, for the generation of electric power, and for scientific and medical research.

These memories of my time at the Naval Academy are especially vivid for me. My impression is that I enjoyed it all, even the less pleasant parts. It was a time of challenge, excitement, and learning.

Assignments for Annapolis graduates were based on priorities determined by drawing lots. My name was drawn almost last, so I got almost the last choice. Luckily, my assignment turned out, nonetheless, to be one of the more interesting ones. For two years I worked on experimental radar and gunnery ships operating out of Norfolk. I was the officer in charge of the education of enlisted men at the high-school and college levels, and also the electronics and photography officer.

The postwar navy was in bad shape. It was a time of great discouragement because we were undermanned, the nation was relaxing after a long and difficult war, and funds allocated for naval operations were meager. I became most disillusioned with the navy, and the military in general, and probably would have resigned had not I and all Annapolis graduates been serving "at the pleasure of the President." Reenlistments in the navy were rare, and most of the ships which remained in commission were understaffed. Sea operations were curtailed, and morale was low.

I was assigned to the USS *Wyoming,* a former old battleship converted into an electronics and gunnery experimental vessel. Prototypes of new navigation, radar, fire control, communication,

The new Annnapolis graduate, Jimmy Carter

and gunnery equipment were installed on the *Wyoming*. We oper-ated out of Norfolk to test the new ideas at sea. In addition to reg-ular line-officer duties, I learned to repair electronic equipment, to conduct photographic analysis of gunnery accuracy using 35 mm motion-picture cameras, and to assess statistically the perfor-mance of radar, guns, gyroscopic compasses, and navigation and radio equipment. The work was interesting, but the duty was ter-rible. We were at sea most of the time with only about two-thirds of a normal crew.

When we were in port, my crew was responsible for moving, installing, and modifying the items to be tested the next week. To compound the problems, our good ship *Wyoming* was declared to be unsafe and was not permitted to tie up at the Norfolk Navy Yard piers. We had to anchor on the far side of the harbor. I sel-dom saw my new bride.

After about a year, the USS *Mississippi* replaced the decrepit

As a navy officer assigned to submarine duty

Wyoming as the navy's seagoing experiment station. As the two years of required surface-ship duty drew to a close, I began to consider the possibilities for my future in the navy. My wife, Rosalynn, and I chose submarines as the best opportunity for purposeful service. I applied and was accepted for submarine duty, and in the summer of 1948 we moved to New London, Connecticut, for a six-month officer training school.

I always found the submarine force to be exciting and challenging, and the next five years proved to be one of the most interesting and enjoyable periods of my life. The crew and officers lived in intimate contact with one another, depending upon the quality of each man and his knowledge of the ship to provide safety and effectiveness for us all. There was an elite group at the submarine school, and the competition was intense. The instructors in New London were proud submariners themselves, and our mock battles were compared to actual submarine actions during the Second World War.

We had to learn in meticulous detail the various systems which comprised a fleet-type submarine—fuel oil, fresh water, hydraulic, high-pressure and low-pressure air, electricity, communications, diesel engines, electrical motors, radar, sonar, fire control, torpedo, gunnery, and dozens of subsystems. Rescue drills were conducted in a tremendous water tank. We would enter the bottom of the tank through airlocks and then rise individually through one hundred feet of water to the surface, breathing into a "Momsen" lung. Later we made one-hundred-foot free ascents without the lung.

There were sixty-one officers in my submarine class in New London. We were there in the fall of 1948 during the national elections. I was the only one who openly supported Harry Truman for president.

After graduation in December of 1948, Rosalynn and I drove our first car, a Studebaker, down to Plains. She and our son Jack stayed there with our parents, and I took the car to Los Angeles, shipped it to Hawaii, and then flew out to join the USS *Pomfret* (SS 391), my first submarine.

We left for the Far East two days later. That first trip of mine to the Far East occurred during one of the major storms of Pacific Ocean history. I was seasick for five straight days. Several ships were lost, and once I almost lost my own life.

The ship had to be on the surface during the time we were recharging batteries each night, so that the diesel engines could get air to run. This was before the days of snorkeling for United States submarines. In the middle of one night—during a heavy storm—we were on the surface, and I was on the submarine bridge about fifteen feet above the level of the ocean itself, holding on as tightly as I could to an iron pipe handrail inside the bridge shield.

An enormous wave rose around us to a level of about six feet or so above my head. I lost my grip as the force of the wave tore my hand from the handrail, and I found myself swimming literally within the huge wave, completely separated from the submarine itself.

After I swam for a good while—it seemed forever—the wave receded, and I landed on top of the five-inch gun located about thirty feet aft of where I had been standing. I clung desperately to the gun barrel, and finally was able to lower myself to the deck and return to my watch station. Had the currents been even slightly broadside instead of from forward to aft, I never would have landed on the ship as the wave receded, and would undoubtedly have been lost at sea in the dark storm.

Our radio transmitting equipment was drowned out by the pounding salt water, and we could not send our daily location report to Pacific Fleet Headquarters. There was a normal procedure under which the shore station would try to call us after a certain interval of time passed without our having reported our position. We could hear their calls but could not answer, and we changed course and turned toward Midway, so we might report that our ship had not been lost.

One final message received by us in that period, one which I shall always remember, was this: "To all ships in the Pacific (in that area). Be on the lookout for floating debris left by submarine USS *Pomfret,* believed to have been sunk approximately seven hundred miles south of Midway Island."

At this point, we began desperately trying to reach a communications point to notify the navy and our families that we were not lost. Other wives living in Hawaii were notified that our submarine may have sunk, but Rosalynn fortunately did not know about this occurrence at the time, because she was back in Georgia with young Jack.

When I could finally stand up below decks without throwing up, I began to learn the ship. Every pipe, fitting, valve, switch, hatch, control, and lever had to be known intimately, so that in times of emergency instantaneous decisions could be made about the proper operation of each system in the submarine. Our lives were so interdependent, dependent on every man knowing his job, that no lack of enthusiasm was tolerated as we studied all aspects of submarine operation, patrol, and warfare. Any member of a crew who was lackadaisical about learning the ship was promptly transferred to the surface fleet.

We spent a couple of months along the China coast between Hong Kong and Tsingtao. It was an extremely interesting time. Ours and the British navy ships operating out of mainland China ports always tied up at the piers with bows pointed toward the harbor exit to permit quick departure. Chinese Communist troops were surrounding the cities, and their campfires could be seen in the hills. Shop windows were boarded up, and standard goods such as raw silk, carved wood, and ivory were cheap. The people were nervous and tense. Nationalist troops conscripted very young and old "volunteers" at bayonet point, and on one occasion soldiers fired at a jeep which was being used by our ship's captain. One bullet went through the canvas roof.

We operated in the Yellow Sea as a target so that U.S. and British surface ships could practice their anti-submarine warfare skills. I was proud to be in the submarine force and considered the *Pomfret* and her crew to be the best in the navy.

During these war-game exercises, we were on duty four hours and then off duty for four hours; we performed all of our many regular chores during the off-duty hours. This routine was followed for days at a time, but we were in high spirits, and any complaints made—and there were many—seemed offered merely to uphold the navy tradition.

We spent a year and a half operating out of Pearl Harbor. A few months after our second son, Chip, was born in April 1950, the *Pomfret* was transferred back to San Diego.

In 1950 the navy decided to build its first new ship since the end of World War II, and I was ordered to report to New London as the senior officer of the precommissioning detail. The ship was a comparatively small, extremely quiet submarine which was designed exclusively to fight in the quiet depths of the sea against other submerged vessels.

This ship, the USS *K-1* was designed and constructed at the Electric Boat Company in New London, Connecticut, and my responsibility there was to represent the navy in the installation, assessment, and sometimes the redesign of various components which went into this new type of submarine.

In fact, I was the only navy person on the ship for several months and enjoyed the engineering work during the final assembly stages of the boat. Long-range listening sonar and other new equipment were installed on the *K-1*. I was also responsible for the evolution of the various procedures which would be used when the

The USS K-1, *antisubmarine submarine*

ship ultimately went to sea, including engineering, maintenance, diving and surfacing, development of personnel billets, and projected supply requirements.

Other more senior officers were later assigned to the *K-1* when time for actual commissioning approached, and all the men then learned together the operating procedures before we went to sea, including those for diving, surfacing, hovering, and other maneuvers.

I was intrigued with the innovative and experimental nature of this work. The *K-1* performed well and contributed a great deal to the knowledge of undersea sound transmission, making possible an analysis of enemy ship movements by monitoring various noises at long range.

We would stay submerged for long periods of time, working in stockinged feet with no machinery in operation, controlling our depth simply by raising or lowering the periscope a few inches at a time. With a constant ship weight and a slightly varying amount of water displaced, the submarine would rise or sink very slowly as the periscope was moved. This fine balance took a lot of skill, experience, and luck, but gave us a platform of almost complete silence from which to listen to our prospective targets. We could hear all kinds of strange sea-creature sounds and could detect other ships at extraordinary distances.

During our shakedown cruise near Provincetown, Massachusetts, we fired a practice torpedo which surfaced as programmed at the end of its run. One of the fishing boats was trying to recover the torpedo as it bobbed up and down in the waves, and on one bob upward the torpedo knocked a large hole in the side of the boat. The boat began to sink and had to be run up on the beach. This was the first (and only) USS *K-1* "kill."

Once, after we had been submerged for about three weeks, one of our electrician's mates went mad with claustrophobia. We fed him intravenously and strapped him in a bunk to restrain him, which I am sure did not help his affliction. We finally had to surface, and transferred him to a helicopter a few hundred miles south of Bermuda. He never went back on a submarine.

The duty was tough, dangerous, and demanding. Yet we submariners liked the service, enjoyed the physical and personal closeness, and were proud of the high standards and professional demands made on us.

While serving on the *K-1*, I was qualified to command submarines, but I was never senior enough while in the navy to have a ship of my own. My command thesis described a new technique for determining the distance to a target ship, using information derived from the passive listening equipment only.

FIVE

Why Not the Best?

Navy Admiral Hyman Rickover is by any measure a remarkable man.

In 1949, because of the admiral's prodding, the navy made a commitment to develop a nuclear propulsion plant for ships, and then contracted with two major companies to build prototype atomic-powered submarines. Westinghouse began to design and build the power plant for the submarine *Nautilus*, which would use "liquid water" to bring the heat out of the nuclear reactor core. General Electric at the same time began to construct the power plant for the *Sea Wolf*, which would use liquid sodium, instead of water, as the heat transfer agent.

As soon as I heard about this program, I applied for assignment to what I considered the finest navy billet available to any officer of my rank—the development of the first atomic submarines.

After a screening interview with then-Captain Rickover, I was ordered to Schenectady, New York, as senior officer of the crew of the *Sea Wolf*, and began to teach the men mathematics, physics, and reactor technology. At the same time, we helped the General Electric workers to construct the prototype power plant within a huge steel sphere near Knolls Atomic Power Laboratory. Another officer, Charles Carlisle, and I studied special graduate courses in reactor technology and nuclear physics at Union College.

We took the enlisted men from simple fractions through differential equations within a year. We all thoroughly combined our theoretical studies with daily practical applications of our knowledge in the building of the first nuclear propulsion components.

All of us had high security clearances, and we traveled a lot from Schenectady to the Atomic Energy Commission headquarters in Washington, D.C., to the Hanford Works in Washington State where plutonium was made, and to Idaho where the *Nautilus* prototype was built and experimental reactors were operated. We had confidence in the safety of the reactors which we studied and operated. So far as I know, only one nuclear reactor ever went out of control, and it was an experimental installation located at Chalk River, Canada. It melted, and some radioactive material did escape into the atmosphere, but no one was injured.

Later, because of our security clearance and experience in the field, we were asked to go to this Canadian site to help in disassembling the damaged nuclear reactor core. The radiation intensity meant that each person could spend only about ninety seconds at the hot core location.

An exact duplicate mock-up of the reactor was constructed on a nearby tennis court, and television cameras monitored the actual damaged equipment far beneath the ground. Each time our men managed to remove a bolt or fitting from the core, the equivalent piece was removed on the mock-up.

When it was our time to work, a team of three of us practiced several times on the mock-up to be sure we had the correct tools and knew exactly how to use them. Finally, outfitted with white protective clothes, we descended into the reactor and worked frantically for our allotted time.

For several months afterward, we saved our feces and urine to have them monitored for radioactivity. We had absorbed a year's maximum allowance of radiation in one minute and twenty-nine seconds. There were no apparent aftereffects from this exposure—just a lot of doubtful jokes among ourselves about death versus sterility.

During this early period of atomic submarine development, I worked with a relatively small group of naval officers who had a joint responsibility to the submarine force and to the Atomic Energy Commission. We had an unorthodox organization wherein rank or seniority was of little importance.

Captain Rickover and four junior officers had been involved

in the nuclear program for five or six years, having been sent to Oak Ridge, Tennessee, at the beginning of the program in 1946. Rickover is probably the most competent and innovative naval engineer of all time, but the hidebound Navy Selection Board passed him over twice for promotion in the early 1950s, which made mandatory retirement seem inevitable. He was finally promoted and retained in the naval service only after President Truman and influential members of Congress directly intervened to save his naval career.

He may not have cared or known it, certainly not at that time, but Admiral Rickover had a profound effect on my life—perhaps more than anyone except my own parents.

He was unbelievably hardworking and competent, and he demanded total dedication from his subordinates. We feared and respected him and strove to please him. I do not in that period remember his ever saying a complimentary word to me. The absence of a comment was his compliment; he never hesitated to criticize severely if a job were not done as well as he believed it could be done. He expected the maximum from us, but he always contributed more.

Once I remember flying to Seattle with him at the end of a hard day's work. It was a long flight in the commercial prop-jet plane. He began to work when the plane took off, and we were determined to do the same. After a few hours the rest of us gave up and went to sleep. When we awoke, Rickover was still working.

He was never tactful or timid in his demands upon the Congress, the navy, or the manufacturers who supplied the thousands of equipment parts of unprecedented design. Executives of the companies realized that Admiral Rickover often knew more about their construction capabilities and schedules than they did. His ships were generally built on time, and the power plants performed better than expected. What could have been a terrible failure and a series of boondoggles turned out to be a notable success and a source of pride for the nation.

Admiral Rickover's career has been brilliant and remarkable, equal in significance in U.S. Naval history to that of the great engineers who played a critical role when the U.S. Navy made the transition to steam power near the end of the nineteenth century. Rickover served at sea after his graduation from Annapolis in 1922, taking graduate work in electrical engineering at Annapolis and at Columbia during the 1920s. That specialized background led him to become head of the electrical division of the Navy Department's Bureau of Ships during World War II. It was after the war (and after a six-month tour of duty as assistant director of operations of the Manhattan Engineering District at Oak Ridge, Tennessee, in 1946) that Rickover became convinced of the imperative military need of developing an atomic-powered submarine.

He managed to win appointment as head of the atomic submarine division of the Bureau of Ships in 1947 and then battled tirelessly, never without criticism, to develop and construct and perfect our first atomic submarines. He was later instrumental in the development of the first atomic reactors for generating electrical power and for propelling surface ships including aircraft carriers. Rickover, far more than any other single man, deserves credit for these achievements and for this part of the development of the nation's modern navy.

He always insisted that we know our jobs in the most minute detail, which is really a necessary basic characteristic of good submariners. He was often appalled at the incompetence of leaders who knew the theory of management but knew little about what actually occurred within their sphere of responsibility. He has been very critical of our nation's educational system, and particularly of the Naval Academy because of the graduates' inability to assume technical responsibility for specific naval duties. He believes they should concentrate on engineering, mathematics, and other technical courses so that they can understand the ships they are assigned to operate.

As he has pointed out, the growing bureaucracy of the military establishment is an obstacle to an adequate defense for our nation. As a full admiral responsible for naval nuclear propulsion, Rickover has had twenty-one intermediate authorities between him and the Secretary of Defense. Each of the twenty-one could veto or delay a proposal, but none could give final approval.

Incidentally, there was only one intermediary between Rickover and the chairman of the Atomic Energy Commission.

Rickover did not play a prominent role in the ceremonies when the keel of the *Nautilus* was laid in New London in 1952. President Truman was the center of attention.

After the ceremony, driving back to Schenectady, Rosalynn and I reviewed again my first meeting with this iconoclastic navy figure who had overcome all obstacles and was about to prove that the awesome power of atomic fission could be harnessed to propel a ship—and not just to kill.

I had applied for the nuclear submarine program, and Admiral Rickover was interviewing me for the job. It was the first time I met Admiral Rickover, and we sat in a large room by ourselves for more than two hours, and he let me choose any subject I wished to discuss. Very carefully, I chose those about which I knew most at the time—current events, seamanship, music, literature, naval tactics, electronics, gunnery—and he began to ask me a series of questions of increasing difficulty. In each instance, he soon proved that I knew relatively little about the subject I had chosen.

He always looked right into my eyes, and he never smiled. I was saturated with cold sweat.

Finally, he asked me a question, and I thought I could redeem myself. He said, "How did you stand in your class at the Naval Academy?" Since I had completed my sophomore year at Georgia Tech before entering Annapolis as a plebe, I had done very well, and I swelled my chest with pride and answered, "Sir, I stood fifty-ninth in a class of 820!" I sat back to wait for the congratulations —which never came. Instead, the question: "Did you do your best?" I started to say, "Yes, sir," but I remembered who this was, and recalled several of the many times at the Academy when I could have learned more about our allies, our enemies, weapons, strategy, and so forth. I was just human. I finally gulped and said, "No, sir, I didn't *always* do my best."

He looked at me for a long time, and then turned his chair around to end the interview. He asked one final question, which I have never been able to forget—or to answer. He said, "Why not?" I sat there for a while, shaken, and then slowly left the room.

I worked for Rickover until 1953, when my father died of cancer. I was permitted to go home on leave during his terminal illness, and I spent hours by his bedside. We talked about old times together and about those intervening eleven years when we had rarely seen each other.

Hundreds of people came by to speak to Daddy or to bring him a choice morsel of food or some fresh flowers. It was obvious that he meant much to them, and it caused me to compare my prospective life with his. After his funeral, I went back to Schenectady.

I began to think about the relative significance of his life and mine. He was an integral part of the community and had a wide range of varied but interrelated interests and responsibilities. He was his own boss, and his life was stabilized by the slow and evolutionary changes in the local societal structure.

My job was the best and most promising in the navy, and the work was challenging and worthwhile. The salary was good, and the retirement benefits were liberal and assured. The contact with Admiral Rickover alone made it worthwhile.

But after some torturous days, I decided to resign from the navy and come home to Plains—to a tiny town, a church, a farm, an uncertain income. I had only one life to live, and I wanted to live it as a civilian, with a potentially fuller opportunity for varied public service.

SIX

Back Home Again

It was the first serious argument in our marriage.

My wife, Rosalynn, simply did not agree that we should leave the navy and return to Plains, and it was with mixed feelings that we made the decision.

Now I want to explain what we did and write a little about my family, especially Rosalynn—and about trying to start a business, and about the kinds of economic, social, and cultural issues that could confront a white man, a farmer, in a small Southern town in the 1950s and early 1960s.

The Carter family cemetery is located a few miles north of Plains, and the first person buried there was Wiley Carter, born in 1798. My ancestors moved into the area from northeast Georgia shortly after the Indians moved out around 1830. Rosalynn's family cemetery is located a few miles south of Plains, and her first ancestor to live there, Drury Murray, was born in 1787. Both of these early settlers died during the War between the States. Our children will be the sixth generation to own the same land.

When I was a child, my daddy's mother, Nina, lived in Plains in a large house by herself, and one of her several grandchildren was assigned to spend the night with her each night of the week. Friday became my regular night after I was about eight years old. My grandmother was very pretty, quite old-fashioned, vain about her age and appearance, and made a pleasant companion, at least for that one night each week.

On those Friday evenings, we would play Tin Can, hide-and-seek, and similar games under the street lights. It was there and at school that I began to know the girls who lived in Plains. I had my first date with Grandma's next-door neighbor when I was thirteen years old and used the family pickup truck on that occasion for the first time by myself (although I had driven it regularly on the farm roads).

There were two or three girls that I liked from time to time in high school and college. But I never had any real sweetheart, and in fact never told any girl that I loved her. Just before I began my last year at Annapolis, I was at home in Plains completing my summer leave period and late one afternoon was cruising around in a rumble-seated Ford with a friend of mine. We saw my sister Ruth and another girl in the churchyard and stopped to talk with them. The other girl was Rosalynn Smith, several years younger than I, who had been around our home a few times with Ruth. I had never paid much attention to her, but we asked the two girls for a movie date, and they accepted.

I returned home later that night and told my mother that Rosalynn had gone to the movies with me. Mother asked if I liked her, and I was already sure of my answer when I replied, "She's the girl I want to marry." Rosalynn has never had any competition for my love.

The next Christmas we saw each other every night. I asked Rosalynn if she would marry me, but she said NO. Later, at Annapolis on Washington's birthday holiday, she finally accepted my proposal. We set a date for our July wedding.

We were married in the Plains Methodist Church a month after my graduation. It was a relatively informal wedding, almost more informal than anyone planned. I had always been punctual in the navy, rarely ever late for anything. On our wedding day the ceremony was scheduled for three in the afternoon, and I picked Rosalynn up at her mother's house at a quarter before the hour, knowing that we were in good time as we drove up into the churchyard. Yet, just as we arrived, we heard the pianist, whose watch was apparently five minutes fast, playing the last notes of "Here Comes the Bride." We dashed out of the car and up the church steps. The pianist played the song a second time as we entered the church for the brief ceremony.

We rented an apartment in Norfolk, Virginia, where I was assigned to my first ship, the *Wyoming*, and later to the *Mississippi*.

While Rosalynn and I were in Norfolk, I worked at sea all week and one-third of my weekends. So, on two out of three weekends, when there were no special responsibilities on the ship, I was able to be home Saturday afternoon and Sunday. This meant that Rosalynn had to manage all the affairs of our home, as she has continued to do ever since. Money was scarce. My ensign's salary was $300 per month, out of which we paid $100 for rent, $54 for my food on the ship, and $75 for a war bond. That left $71 for all other expenses in a month's time. Rosalynn has always handled responsibility well. She has a strong will of her own (which has seemed to get stronger with each passing year).

Our first son was born in the Portsmouth Navy Hospital in July of 1947, about a year after we were married. We named him John William, after Rosalynn's grandfather, and called him Jack.

After finishing the two years at sea out of Norfolk, I was accepted for submarine duty, and we moved to New London, Connecticut, for submarine school. Then, in the winter of 1948, I was assigned to my first submarine, based in Pearl Harbor in the Hawaiian Islands.

Rosalynn and Jack stayed behind in Plains and waited until it was time for me to return from the Far East to Honolulu, and then met me there about a week after I returned to the islands in April of 1949.

Our married life in the navy was one of constant separations interspersed with ecstatic reunions and the melding of ourselves over the years into a closer relationship of love, understanding, and mutual respect.

The islands of Hawaii were relatively undeveloped and unspoiled in those years around 1950. On Oahu there were no buildings at all between the Royal Hawaiian Hotel and Diamond Head. Living was relatively inexpensive, and Rosalynn and I thoroughly enjoyed our almost two-year stay in what seemed to be an ocean paradise. Our second son, James Earl, was born in Tripler Hospital on the island of Oahu. The hospital nurses called him "Chip," and Chip he has been ever since.

After the Korean War began, our submarine was ordered back to San Diego for duty there, operating from a submarine tender anchored in the bay. This seaport was crowded with military personnel, and we had difficulty finding a place to stay. Most of our neighbors were immigrants from nearby Mexico and, because I was at sea so much, Rosalynn often felt isolated in the civilian community. We visited Tijuana on occasion, and we were able to practice our Spanish during those visits and also with our Spanish-speaking neighbors in San Diego.

My mother and father visited us in the fall of 1950. While they were there I received orders to be in charge of precommissioning work on the USS K-1. We lived in New London until the ship was commissioned, and during that period our third son, Jeffrey, was born in Connecticut.

Most of our friends and neighbors were in the navy, but our growing family gave us more intimate contact within the civilian communities where we lived. The churches, kindergartens, and athletic events all tended to expand our lives beyond the bounds of the tight navy community.

Our new experimental submarine operated primarily off the New England coast, but on occasion made trips to the deeper and warmer waters of the Caribbean. When we were transferred to the atomic submarine program, my assignment took us to Schenectady, New York, where we spent the remainder of my naval career.

We had many mild family arguments, but the first major disagreement between Rosalynn and me came after my father's funeral. When I came back to Schenectady and told her that I would like to resign from the navy, she disagreed violently. She did not, she protested, wish to go back to the restrictive life of our home in Plains, where our families lived and where our married freedom might be cramped or partially dominated by relatives, particularly her mother and my mother.

However, Rosalynn reluctantly agreed. I finally resigned from the navy, and we went back home in the winter of 1953.

We had saved a few thousand dollars from our regular Savings Bonds program since my Annapolis days. Though we felt young and confident, we had no idea what our life would be like when we returned home.

Not having any assured income, we applied for—and were assigned—an apartment in the new public-housing project in Plains. I remember that on the way home from Schenectady we stopped in Washington to visit our congressman, Mr. "Tic" Forrester. He was an extremely small man physically, cocky, and constantly preoccupied with the question of civil rights. He showed us around the Capitol building and, in one of his apparently standard speeches, described to us the problem of living near people who occupied public-housing quarters. Rosalynn and I glanced at one another, but did not comment.

Our return to Plains was not a momentous event for the community in any way that I can recall.

Jeffrey was still a baby. Chip was three years old. Jack was a first grader. We began a modest business enterprise in partnership with my mother during the 1954 growing season—a season which turned out to be one of the worst drought years in the history of Georgia. That also, as it happened, was the year of the U.S. Supreme Court decision concerning racial integration of public schools.

We had a total profit for that first year in business of less than two hundred dollars. I was my own—and only—employee and during the season sold about two thousand tons of fertilizer in one-hundred-pound paper bags or in two-hundred-pound burlap bags. I loaded the bags myself, sometimes with the help of the farmer customers. At that time, farmers ordinarily bought their fertilizer one ton at a time and loaded it on pickup trucks going directly to the fields where crops were being planted.

All this was quite a change from the navy, but we never felt that it had been a mistake to return home. At first I knew little about business and had forgotten much of what I had learned on the farm about growing crops. Also, farming techniques had changed very rapidly since my early days. In any case my understanding of agriculture was completely outdated.

But I was an eager student, and the fact that my economic life depended on my success in learning how to farm helped me in my

Jimmy, Rosalynn, and their three sons, Chip, Jack, and Jeff

studies. I read books, had long talks with the county agent, talked to my father's brother Alton, observed the experienced farmers, and went to short courses at the Agricultural Experiment Station in Tifton, Georgia. I learned rapidly.

I finally mustered enough courage during 1954 to go to the local bank to ask for a small loan. It was refused. We began to grow certified seed peanuts and, in spite of some early setbacks, over a period of years our business expanded well enough.

One of the challenging aspects of my life in Plains revolved around our attitudes toward the race question. During the 1950s, there was strong concern and excitement in Georgia about the Supreme Court rulings and the prospective passage of laws in Congress to eliminate the legal aspects of segregation. I was quite concerned about this problem myself. My views on the subject were sometimes at odds with those of most of my neighbors.

It seems hard to believe now, but I was actually a member of

Unloading peanuts

the county school board for several months before it dawned on me that white children rode buses to their schools and black students still walked to theirs! I don't believe any black parent or teacher ever pointed out this quite obvious difference. Of course, I presume the perceived threat of integration made us—the white citizens—begin to question the "equal" in order to preserve the "separate" public schools for white and black youngsters.

One of the ideas that swept the South in that time was the formation of White Citizens' Councils, most often organized by present or former political leaders who ultimately pocketed large sums of money paid in as dues by irate white citizens.

When the White Citizens' Council movement hit Plains, recruitment of new members did not prove to be difficult. After a few days I was visited by two of the town's leading citizens acting as organizers for the new local White Citizens' Council. One was our chief of police, and the other the local railroad depot agent, who happened also to be a Baptist preacher. I informed them that I did not wish to join the White Citizens' Council.

After some discussion, the two men left, but in a couple of days they returned to my office at the warehouse to notify me that every white male adult in the community had joined the White Citizens' Council . . . except me. I repeated my statement that I did not wish to join, and eventually they left again.

After a few more days, they came back with several of my close friends, some of whom were customers of mine in the seed and fertilizer business. They pointed out that it would damage my reputation and my success as a businessman in the community if I proved to be the only holdout in the community, and because of their genuine concern about my welfare they were willing to pay the dues for me.

My response was that I had no intention of joining the organization on any basis, that I was willing to leave Plains if necessary, that the five dollar dues requirement was not an important factor, and that I would never change my mind. Rosalynn and I became quite troubled about our future.

A small boycott was organized against me, but it proved to be short-lived, with one or two minor exceptions. Eventually that altercation, which seemed to us so important at the time, faded into insignificance.

There was also a serious problem with the churches in the community, brought into focus by the concerted effort of the more activist civil-rights groups to integrate the white church congregations. There were several public confrontations in nearby Americus, at the more prominent Methodist and Baptist churches.

In our own church at Plains, we had historically invited black neighbors to attend special services like weddings, funerals, and sometimes baptisms, but it had not been the custom for many years for blacks to attend the regular worship services. Earlier in the history of our little church, following the War between the States, black and white worshipers attended the same services, but then the churches split into separate congregations, and from that time forward they were segregated.

I was a deacon in our church and missed one very critical deacons' meeting during this period. On that occasion, the other eleven deacons and our pastor voted unanimously to propose to the church congregation that if any blacks attempted to enter the church on Sunday they would be blocked and excluded from the worship service. I heard about this vote later, after the meeting, and it disturbed me deeply.

On the Saturday before our monthly church conference, my family and I were attending the wedding of a cousin of mine north of Atlanta. All the members of my family were there for the wedding. I was already a state senator and was preparing to run for higher office, and Rosalynn and I discussed the consequences of creating an argument in church about the deacons' proposal to exclude blacks from the worship services. We talked about my political ambitions, future career, and the advisability of avoiding controversy at that time.

We finally decided to get up early and drive home to the church on that Sunday morning of the conference. Ordinarily, there were only about thirty-five people attending the monthly conference, but that morning there were about two hundred people present. I asked for recognition and spoke to members of the church urging them to reverse the decision of the deacons—and of the pastor—and to permit free entry of any blacks who attempted to enter our church—as long as their motives seemed peaceful, and if they seemed to be there not simply to provoke a confrontation but to take part in our worship services.

There were several opposing arguments, and then came the vote. The only six people voting to keep the services open to all worshipers were my mother, my wife, Rosalynn, our two sons, myself, and one other member of the congregation.

But only about fifty people voted on the other side, in favor of sustaining the deacons' position. Many other church members did not vote. Later, several dozen of them told me that they agreed with my stand, but did not want to vote openly in the church conference.

Hopefully, not many churches in the United States today would forcibly exclude any worshiper because of race, but this was a hotly debated issue throughout the South in the 1960s. Physical violence erupted even in the entrances of several larger Atlanta churches—churches whose deacons, on the whole, must have felt the same as the deacons in our church in Plains.

The significance of these two incidents—my experience with the White Citizens' Council recruiting effort and in my own church—is still hard for me to assess. In each instance there was a small group of extremely fervent advocates of maintaining the strictest racial segregation. My own belief, in retrospect, is that a majority of the members of the community chose, perhaps reluctantly, to abide by the law in a quiet and unobtrusive manner. In either instance, there were never any serious adverse consequences for my action or for the attitudes of my own family.

As the civil-rights movement gathered momentum in the South in the 1960s, personal conflicts began to develop within the white community. Some public leaders profited financially and politically from the formation of such groups as the Citizens' Council. The boycott attempt on my embryonic business was interesting because it failed. It failed in part because many of my white customers resented being pressured into paying dues into the coffers of a nonfunctioning organization. It would be illuminating even today to know what ever happened to all of the money collected for White Citizens' Councils throughout the South!

The early expressed commitments to close all our public schools and colleges rather than integrate began to wane when the consequences of uneducated children began to be seriously assessed. A common and independent decision was made by hundreds of white school board members to yield to federal court orders. Private schools absorbed the children of unyielding white parents. Perhaps these private schools were not without value in a difficult time, serving in a way as community safety valves. It took some time, but the provisions of other civil-rights laws were also finally accepted.

It was a trying era in the South as the social and political patterns of a century were changed almost overnight.

Most of the citizens of Georgia and other Southern states, at least those in rural areas, had lived in intimate, personal contact with their neighbors—both black and white—in the factories, in the fields, in trade and commerce, in prosperity, and in hardship and sorrows. And there were curiously easy personal relationships (segregation notwithstanding). Both black and white Southerners, to a great extent, had a better understanding of each other, of attitudes and customs, than black and white Americans in other parts of the country.

Ivan Allen Jr. was the mayor of Atlanta in a controversial time, through most of the troubled 1960s. He drew on—and profited from—the history in Atlanta of strong leadership from both black and white communities. There was one occasion in that period when a chamber of commerce delegation from a large Northern city came to city hall in Atlanta and wanted to talk about Atlanta's experience of good race relations. Mayor Allen arranged a meeting in his office with four black Atlanta leaders. The visitors, all white businessmen, wanted advice about their own city and found, to their surprise, that the black Atlantans knew by name several important black leaders in that Northern city, leaders the visitors did not know, even by name! In the South, this hardly could have happened. White and black citizens lived and worked too closely together in most communities.

The striking down of legal barriers between citizens gave us an opportunity to capitalize on these long-existing personal relationships. It is for this reason, I think, that the transition from a segregated to an integrated society in the South has been much less traumatic than had been predicted by many during those early years.

After our return to Plains, in our second year home, Rosalynn began coming to the office one day each week to help with the books and with the preparation of invoices. Later she began to come half of each day, and finally she studied bookkeeping and began working fulltime at the warehouse with me. We have been full partners in every major decision since we first married.

When we decided to enter politics, Rosalynn helped me from every standpoint. Later, when I ran for governor, she became an extremely effective campaigner on her own, shaking hands with tens of thousands of Georgia voters from before daybreak until after midnight. She was hesitant about it at first, but later became a fine public speaker, able to express forcefully her deep concerns about the social responsibilities of a government to its people, particularly in the field of mental health, her special interest.

The personal abuse, which I guess is an inherent part of all political life, has always bothered Rosalynn more than it has me or my sons. Yet, her judgment on political matters is sound, and her instant analysis of the sincerity of political persons is almost infallible.

Our oldest son, Jack, has a degree from Georgia Tech in nuclear physics and finished law school at the University of Georgia in June of 1975. Our second son, Chip, is living in Plains and was recently elected to the city council. Both their wives are elementary school teachers. Our youngest son, Jeff, is a student at Georgia State University, and his wife has her degree in interior decorating.

All of our sons have been active in my campaigns for the governorship, and all three have worked with me in the governor's office during different legislative sessions, serving in strategic roles without pay.

I have always loved children; I wish Rosalynn and I had ten of them. Yet, after we returned to Plains from the navy, we found that Rosalynn had some physical problems which prevented her from having another child. It was more than a dozen years later when an operation became necessary to remove a large tumor from her uterus. After that operation, Rosalynn's obstetrician said that she could have another child. We began to pray for a daughter.

Amy came.

It was after twenty-one years of marriage and fifteen years after Jeffrey was born. Amy has made us young again, rebound our family together, and been a source of joy, pride, and delight. Her three brothers are so much older that it is almost as though she has four fathers, and we have had to stand in line to spoil her.

Amy was three years old when we moved into the governor's mansion in early 1971, and she has had a rapidly developing life among adults. She is probably the most famous member of our family, being interviewed and photographed continually at a young age and being actively involved in all sorts of state activities.

My brother, Billy, reminds me of my father—in appearance, habits, and attitudes. When we returned home from the navy, Billy was only sixteen years old, and not at all inclined to take orders from an older brother. As soon as he finished high school, he left to join the Marine Corps and shortly thereafter married his childhood sweetheart, Sybil Spires. A few years later they came back home to live. Billy became a partner in our business, and now he runs it in my absence. Our friendship has grown steadily with the years, and I realize that his willingness to operate our farms and warehouse has made it possible for me to hold public office.

My youngest sister, Ruth, is a full-time evangelist who travels to different parts of the nation and even the world, expressing in the most refreshing way her deep faith and personal relationship with Christ. She is married to Dr. Robert Stapleton, a veterinarian who was a neighbor of ours in Sumter County. They live in Fayetteville, North Carolina.

My other sister, Gloria, is an art teacher and ardent motorcyclist who, with her husband, Walter Spann, has a home on the outskirts of Plains. Recently, they sold most of their farmland and now live part time in a cabin on the Flint River in the western part of the county.

As the matriarch of our family, my mother, Lillian, provided a nucleus around which our different individual families revolved. She is an extrovert, very dynamic, inquisitive in her attitude about life, compassionate toward others, and has had a wide variety of experiences even in her advancing years.

Mother is a registered nurse and has always been a natural champion for those who were weak or the object of scorn or discrimination. When my father died in 1953, Mother began to evolve a new life. For six years she was a fraternity housemother at Auburn University, and then opened and operated a small nursing home in Blakely, Georgia.

Jimmy, in Plains, with his mother, Lillian Gordy Carter

One night in 1966, when she was sixty-eight years old, she saw a television advertisement for Peace Corps volunteers, which stated "Age is no barrier." She sent off for information and then came in to announce to Billy and me that she was joining the Peace Corps for service in Africa or India. We were not particularly surprised.

She went to the University of Chicago to learn the Indian dialect, Marathi, so she could teach nutrition to the people of India. Then Mrs. Gandhi requested that some of the volunteers be assigned to an experimental program in family planning, and Mother had to learn another language, Hindi.

She went to the small town of Vikhroli, a few miles north of Bombay, and stayed there until her normal tour was completed. Because of her medical knowledge, she was soon transferred part time to a little clinic, where she performed the services of a medical nurse and doctor after her regular family-planning duties were done. Visiting the native homes and counseling people—who had little personal pleasure in life except sex—left her frustrated and unhappy. There were no birth-control devices, and she had to rec-

ommend and almost require continence and vasectomy operations. For instance, no family could send a fourth child to school
or live in public housing unless one of the parents was rendered
infertile by an operation. When she was asked to work full time at
the little hospital, she eagerly accepted this opportunity.

The experiences there changed her life. These are her own
words as recorded by a newsman shortly after her return from India:

"I had one white dress I had taken with me, so I put it on in
lieu of a uniform and I went over there. And what I beheld when
I went in that door! There were forty patients sitting around waiting for the doctor. This doctor saw two hundred to three hundred
patients every day. And I worked. I did everything but fill pre-
scriptions. I did dressings, injections, helped the doctor examine
and diagnose, helped with his 'stitch-'em-ups,' he called them.
What I did then was say to myself, 'I'll make myself indispensable
to him because this is what I want to do.'"

Mother persuaded the factory owner's wife to provide another
clean room as a full-time dispensary, and she and her family back
in this country induced the major drug companies to supply drug
samples for the treatment of the most common ailments.

She had things going her way, and then a little girl with leprosy came in, whose infectious disease caused Mother concern and
really tested her courage and commitment.

As Mother told it, "I had never touched leprosy. I never felt
like I could. What it looks like—in the last stages one is completely eaten—but in the first stages you have black splotches all
over you, and sores. . . . One day this little girl came in. She was
eleven years old and only weighed thirty-two pounds. She was
across her father's shoulder like a sack of flour. I had my own injection room, and the doctor would send the patient to the drug room
for the medicine, and then to me. And there at the top of this
little girl's prescription it had 'leprosy—infectious leprosy.' And I
thought, 'Oh, God, I can't touch her.'

"I told the man to put the little girl on a cot, and he did. I went
back to the doctor's office and told him I thought I'd never be able
to touch leprosy. And I was about to cry. And he said, 'Try. And
if you can't, I'll come in and do it for you.'

"I made up my mind from his office back to mine that I would give it. And I gave that child streptomycin and Vitamin B and B Complex . . . and I washed my hands, and washed them, and washed them, and all the time I was ashamed for washing them. I put alcohol on them, and it was just before lunchtime, and I went home and took a bath and put on clean clothes. And I knew that wouldn't do. I had told the man to bring her back every day so the next day when she came, I just washed my hands.

"And I learned to love her because in the weeks of giving her injections she began to gain, and soon I could give her an injection and just casually wash my hands. But that took a lot of prayer.

"We finally got her in a leprosarium—they have a long list of people waiting—and six months later she came out, and she came running there one day to me and she brought me a flower—all Indians love flowers—and she put her arms around my neck and *kissed* me. And you know, I didn't wash my face or hands."

When she had to leave India, Mother made the factory owner and the doctor hire a native male nurse to replace her, and he swore to take care of her patients. They still write her with such reports as: "Don't worry about your friend the gardener. His asthma is under control."

When she came home from India she looked terrible. She has always been finicky about food, and had lost more than thirty pounds. They let her leave the airplane first, and she was just skin and bones. We ran to her and insisted that she let us push her to the car in a wheelchair, and did it over her objections. We and her grandchildren had put welcome signs all over Plains, and we had prepared to feed her the foods that she had craved most, like chocolate, cheese, and ham. She could not eat it, thinking about her friends in India, and for a long time she would claim that her stomach had shrunk and she was not hungry.

Although when she came home she was past seventy years old, she began speaking to groups about her experiences in the Peace Corps, and related them to our similar needs for personal service in this country. She has made several hundred such speeches. A major portion of her heart is still in India, but she lives a full and useful life wherever she is.

SEVEN

First Politics

It is difficult for me to remember when my interest in politics began. During the Depression years, political decisions in Washington had an immediate and direct effect on our lives. Farm programs, Rural Electrification, Works Progress Administration, Civilian Conservation Corps, and others were of immense personal importance.

My mother's father, Jim Jack Gordy, was active in politics and was considered the most politically knowledgeable man in Webster and Stewart Counties. For a while he lived near us in the Archery community, and he and Daddy kept the political scene thoroughly analyzed. Grandpa never ran for public office himself but was the postmaster during four presidential administrations, and later was federal district revenue officer. This required nimble political footwork because at that time there was no civil service system. To the winners went the spoils.

My grandfather was an avid supporter of Congressman Tom Watson, who was a nationally known populist in his day. As postmaster in nearby Richland, Georgia, my grandfather had been the person who first conceived the idea of the rural free delivery of mail (RFD) and had repeatedly made his proposals to Congressman Watson to implement this idea through federal legislation. When this was finally accomplished, it was one of my grandfather's proudest achievements. When he was long past retirement age, Jim Jack had a doorkeeper's job at the state capitol just to be involved in the political life of Georgia.

Jim Jack Gordy, Jimmy's
maternal grandfather

The first political rally I remember was for Congressman Charles Crisp, who was Speaker of the House of Representatives in Washington and a candidate for the U.S. Senate. Although the members of my family supported Mr. Crisp's archenemy, Tom Watson, and later Senator Richard B. Russell, we went to the kickoff rally for Congressman Crisp because he was a resident of our home county—and we wanted to see the fun. Mr. Crisp's plans went awry. He very carefully delayed the serving of a barbecue lunch until after his speech, wanting his speech to draw the full attention of the crowd. But a new bread-slicing machine had been installed on the fairgrounds for the occasion, and since none of us had ever seen sliced bread before, most of the crowd gathered to watch this process while only a few others listened to the congressman orate.

Daddy always encouraged me to attend the political rallies in surrounding neighborhoods and towns even when he could not go himself. He became more and more involved in politics and community affairs during his life, and the year before his death was elected to the state legislature. My father served only one year, but it was a thrill for him.

While I was a naval officer, my duty took me to Washington every now and then, and I always visited the Senate chambers where Senators Walter F. George and Richard Russell served. Senator Russell was especially interested in the navy's new programs which, on a few occasions, I had a chance to discuss with him. With my job in the Atomic Power Program, I was in Washington more frequently. All of us closely watched the political developments when Admiral Rickover was almost forced out of the navy and then saved by action of President Truman and congressional leaders.

In general, though, my contact with political life was transient and superficial while I was in the navy.

Immediately after my father's death, the political leaders of the county suggested that my mother fill out the remaining year in Daddy's legislative term. When she refused, one of my father's close friends was chosen to take the post, and he served for eight or ten years in the Georgia House of Representatives. I would not have challenged him for the seat, although I thought about it several times during the ensuing years.

Georgia Senate seats rotated among three counties, so that each county elected a state senator for one two-year term and then skipped four years before the process was repeated. The senators were therefore weak and ineffective, and their elections of little consequence.

There seemed, then, little inducement for me to become interested in running for any office. Although my efforts to establish a viable business were almost a full-time job, other opportunities arose for involvement in public affairs. I became state president of the Certified Seed Organization, district governor of Lions International, chairman of our local planning commission, president of the Georgia Planning Association, and served on the county library board and hospital authority.

All of these and similar pursuits had little political significance.

But I was also appointed to fill a vacancy on the Sumter County School Board, and education became a major interest of mine. After a thorough analysis of our school system, we recommended a major consolidation program which required a voter referendum to implement. As chairman of the school board I made speeches around the county in support of the proposal, which finally lost in the rural areas of the county by eighty-eight votes.

It was my first real venture into election politics and campaigning, and the failure of my effort was a stinging disappointment. My own community of Plains would have lost one of its schools, and my neighbors voted overwhelmingly against the school merger proposals. There was considerable bitterness in Plains because of my support of the consolidation proposal.

One year during our annual revival services at our church in Plains, the visiting minister stayed for the week in my mother's home. After the evening service, he and I were discussing public service in its many possible forms. During the conversation I told him that I was considering running for public office. The Georgia Senate was being reapportioned and for the first time would have a permanent membership with substantive and continuing responsibilities.

The pastor was surprised that I would consider going into politics and strongly advised me not to become involved in such a discredited profession. We had a rather heated argument, and he finally asked, "If you want to be of service to other people, why don't you go into the ministry or into some honorable social service work?" On the spur of the moment I retorted, "How would you like to be the pastor of a church with eighty thousand members?" He finally admitted that it was possible to stay honest and at the same time minister to the needs of the eighty thousand citizens of the fourteenth senate district.

It was at the last minute that I decided to run for one of the new Georgia Senate seats, representing seven counties.

My family, my close friends, and I mounted an amateurish, whirlwind campaign within the seven counties of the district. My opponent had previously won the election as a senator within one of the three counties. However, before he could take office the reapportionment ruling had eliminated the old three-county districts which had historically existed in Georgia. There was a lot of sympathy for him because he was denied the office from his previous election victory. He had the established politicians for him. My supporters were mostly young, and newcomers to politics.

On election day I visited as many of the polling places as possible, and everything seemed to be in order until I arrived in Georgetown, a small town on the Chattahoochee River in the extreme western part of the district. It was the only village in Quitman County. There were no voting booths in the courthouse, and all voters were marking their ballots on a table in full view of the voting officials. The local state legislator and dominant political boss of the county was supervising the election—apparently with great interest. Campaign cards of my opponent were on the voting table, and the supervisor would point to the cards and say to each voter, "This is a good man, and my friend." He would watch the ballot being marked and then dropped into a large hole in the top of a pasteboard box, and on several occasions he reached into the box and extracted a few ballots to be examined.

It was an unbelievable scene. He completely ignored my protests. All the other poll workers seemed to obey his orders.

I rode to a cafe and telephoned the newspaper office in the nearby city of Columbus to describe what was occurring. They promised to send a reporter. When I returned after a couple of hours from a visit to another county, the reporter and the political boss were chatting on the steps of the courthouse. It was obvious that they were old friends, and the reporter was not interested in writing any story critical of election procedures in Quitman County. It turned out that the local big shot was an influential employee of the state agriculture department, had complete control over the Democratic Party Election Board, and that his wife ran the county welfare system.

I called John Pope, a friend of mine from my home county, explained what was happening, and asked him to come to Quitman County as an observer. The rest of my day was spent traveling around the district helping my campaign workers get voters to the polls in the other six counties. We obtained the election results by telephone that night at my warehouse office in Plains, and finally I was leading by about seventy votes with the Georgetown box not reported.

We knew that about 300 people had voted there and that the obvious voting irregularities had continued throughout the day. John and several of my Quitman County supporters observed the votes being counted. There were 433 ballots in the box, and according to the names listed, 126 of those voted alphabetically! When the ballots were unfolded, there were sometimes four to eight of them folded together. It was obvious that the box had been stuffed, and I had lost the election by a few votes.

When that report came in, I drove the fifty miles to Georgetown with a young lawyer named Warren Fortson, and we began that night to obtain statements from residents there about the illegal voting procedures that had long been part of their community's political life. We were fighting tough opponents and, during the weeks that followed, our lives were threatened several times. Each time I drove into Georgetown to collect evidence or to obtain affidavits, at least one or two men would silently follow me at a distance of not more than ten feet. They listened to all my conversations and made frequent notes in order to intimidate me and the person I was visiting.

At first, the people were quite timid and reluctant to talk. But we attempted to question everyone who was alleged to have voted. Many of the "voters" were dead, in prison, or had long ago moved away and voted in other communities. Some of the Quitman County citizens were evasive when questioned, and others signed affidavits stating that they had not voted. Our support within the county slowly grew as it became obvious that we were going through with the challenge.

But we were not making any progress with the outside world. The nearby Columbus newspapers pictured me as a politically naive sorehead and a poor loser. State party officials proved to be aloof or downright hostile. The local judge and district attorney had strong ties in the county. Eventually we realized that for years the Quitman County votes had been delivered to state and local candidates in an arbitrary but politically important way. Although few voters were there, the now-illegal county unit system had multiplied Quitman County's significance tenfold.

We presented our challenge to officials at the state Democratic convention in Macon, but it was ignored. My opponent was declared to be the winner, and the official Democratic nominee for the state senate. We could hardly believe it!

Finally we called John Pennington, an investigative reporter for *The Atlanta Journal,* and he quickly joined us in our probe into the Quitman County political corruption. His news stories focused statewide attention on our election challenge. After his publication of the list of voters, dozens of people from around the nation called or wrote to tell us that they had not voted, even though their names were listed.

By the time Pennington began writing his news stories in late October, we had put together about thirty affidavits from voters or observers. My friend John Pope, whom I had asked to go to Georgetown, described what was happening.

"The man who was in charge of the poll in Georgetown on numerous occasions instructed people while they were voting to vote for Moore. During the day I heard him make these remarks to at least 100 voters. . . . For instance, on ballot 122 Rosalyn Moore was repeatedly told that Carter's opponent had already won the election, and he was the home county man and that she should vote for him. I entered the room to observe this closely because the man was speaking in a loud voice. She hesitated for several minutes, saying she just didn't know, and the official stated, 'Just scratch out Carter's name and leave his opponent's.' Rosalyn Moore did as instructed.

"After she left the office I stated again that I didn't think it at all fair for an election officer to try to influence the voters. . . . He told me he would talk to them any ———— way he wanted to, and no one from Americus could come to Georgetown and set down any rules for him to follow."

It was unreal. I talked to that official myself on that election day, and he told me much the same thing: that he had voted for my opponent and would tell all the voters he saw to do likewise.

Warren and I worked day and night to build our case, and my

opponent and his friends began to do the same. There were two struggles, almost unrelated to each other.

One was within Quitman County among the voter registrars, members of the Democratic executive committee, county commissioners, ordinary, sheriff, welfare officials, school superintendent, mayor, aldermen, and the other citizens of the county. Future elections would be decided by the outcome of my investigation and challenges. The other struggle was for the senate seat itself, and involved state and Democratic officials, who at best wanted to avoid the controversy completely.

I almost memorized the Georgia Election Code, and it seemed obvious that almost every section of it had been violated. We learned about many other illegal activities within the community involving moonshine liquor, previous vote frauds, thefts of land, extortion, and other crimes. The threats continued, and so did our investigation.

Eventually we were successful in obtaining a court hearing under the supervision of Judge George Crowe from an adjoining circuit. He was an older man, nearing retirement, who had often expressed his reluctance to change by judicial act the results of a political election. We asked an astute Atlanta attorney, Charles Kirbo, to help us present our case.

When the election officials were finally forced to open the ballot box in the courtroom, its contents had been completely revised. Nothing was as it had been when it was sealed up on election night. All the damaging evidence was simply missing. What we had documented, through observers on the scene, was that only 333 ballots had been officially issued to voters; yet, amazingly, there turned out to be 420 ballots in the box when the votes were counted. Now, again amazingly, all the ballots had vanished entirely.

The officials seemed mystified about who could have done such a thing. While Judge Crowe chewed tobacco, Kirbo made a brief talk about chicken thieves who casually drag a brush behind them to wipe out their own tracks. Then the judge took the case under advisement and adjourned the hearing. He was quoted later as saying, "Under existing election laws, any election can be stolen."

A few days after the hearing Judge Crowe ruled that the Georgetown box was so shot through with fraud that there was no way to determine the intention of any voters, and ordered the election to be decided by the returns from all the other precincts. I was declared the winner. But under a recently passed state law, a technicality was discovered. It permitted an appeal back to the local Democratic executive committee dominated, of course, by the county political boss! My opponent's appeal was predictably successful, and so he was again declared the winner.

Our time was running out. The general election was at hand, and our only hope was a rapid appeal to the state Democratic Party officials, beginning with the party secretary. He was nowhere to be found. Eventually we discovered that he was on a long weekend vacation trip with my opponent's campaign manager!

The state party chairman, J. B. Fuqua, was a nationally prominent industrialist and, then, a complete newcomer to politics. He was hunting pheasant near the Canadian border. Three days before the general election, Kirbo found him, presented our case, and the state party executive committee declared me to be the Democratic nominee.

The secretary of state directed that my name be substituted on the ballots accordingly, and we spent all day Sunday finding the seven county ordinaries and hand stamping all the ballots in preparation for Tuesday's election.

On Monday the other side went into court again, and at midnight, seven hours before the polls opened, the superior court judge ordered the ordinaries to strike all names from the ballot and have a complete new write-in election. Although threatened with contempt of court, two of the county election officials refused to obey the court order, maintaining that their orders concerning elections had to come from the secretary of state.

The election proceeded, with both of us candidates trying to explain to the voters with handbills and radio advertisements what was happening. That night I won by fifteen hundred votes and then went to bed sick and exhausted.

My opponent soon announced that he was challenging the election results because two counties left my name on the ballot.

We prepared to carry the case to the Georgia Senate for a final judgment, but after two or three weeks the challenge was withdrawn, and I finally won.

The local political leader was subsequently convicted in federal court for vote fraud in an earlier election for Congress, and given a three-year suspended sentence. Later he served time for running an illegal liquor distribution operation in Quitman County.

In 1964 our General Assembly passed a comprehensive new election code, primarily as a result of the highly publicized Quitman County scandals in my senate race. Someone suggested as a compromise that no one be allowed to vote who had been dead more than three years!

I really learned a lot from this first experience with politics.

I began to realize how vulnerable our political system was to an accumulation of unchallenged power. Honest and courageous people could be quieted when they came to realize that outspoken opposition was fruitless. Those who were timid and insecure could be intimidated. The dishonest could band together to produce and divide the spoils, and they could easily elect officials who most often seemed respectable but who would cooperate in order to gain a title or office. Jury lists and voter lists could be controlled. Welfare recipients and other dependent people would be aided or deprived. Political favors could be delivered to high officials. And local news media sometimes looked the other way.

But there were other lessons I learned, too. The most vital was that people intimidated by corrupt public officials don't necessarily like it; if given some leadership and a chance, they are willing to stand up and be counted on the side of decency and honest politics and government.

There was another thing I learned. John Pennington wrote in *The Atlanta Journal* some weeks after the election about my friend John Pope. "Mr. Pope," said Pennington, "is not a politician. He is a businessman. He makes burial vaults. He also is an intelligent private citizen with a piercing perceptivity and a strong sense of justice. He is the one man who can be given credit (or blame from those who had been exposed and wish to damn him) for putting his finger on a Georgetown sore spot and holding it there while helping to cause the rest of the state to understand what was going on."

I have thought since then that what was true of John Pope was true, too, of Charlie Kirbo, Warren Fortson, and a host of other people who helped me in that time. None of them helped me in that state senate race controversy for any chance of personal gain. They took on thankless tasks for no other reason than a belief in honesty and in the possibility of the decent, fair handling of the processes of government.

I have found since then that there are countless people all over the country willing to commit themselves in the same way, without thought of personal reward. It sounds old-fashioned, but it is true.

EIGHT

State Senate

When I finally went to the senate in January of 1963, I made what later sometimes seemed an unfortunate pledge—to read every bill before I voted on it.

Although the promise was made originally only to myself, I told several people about it, and for four years I read them all! Each year during Georgia's forty-day legislative session, about twenty-five hundred bills and resolutions are introduced. About half of them come to the floor in one of the houses for a vote, and of these, approximately half are passed into law. I would estimate that in the state senate we voted on eight hundred to one thousand bills during each legislative session. Some are quite brief, yet a few are several hundred pages in length. It was a time-consuming chore, but I took a rapid reading course, and indeed became an expert on many unimportant subjects.

I would go to the state capitol very early every morning and by the time the session began would be familiar with the bills on the calendar. I often detected technical errors and mistakes in the substance of the proposed legislation, also a few shady efforts. One particular legislator introduced many bills each session for all kinds of special interest groups. I amended his bills so often that eventually he would just bring them over, give them to me, and say, "Go through this and cross out what you don't like."

I became a sometimes lonely opponent of "sweetheart" bills which were designed to give some special person a break on salary or retirement benefits. The confusion and complications of state government were almost unbelievable. There were many niches there in which special interests could hide.

I began to work on comprehensive approaches to school finance and education laws, taxation of utilities, scholarship offerings, overcrowded state mental hospitals, election laws, budgeting procedures, and uniform salaries for state officials. It was interesting to introduce a proposal and see who squealed. It became apparent that a lot of confusion was deliberately maintained by those who enjoyed some special privilege. I won some battles and I lost my share. Some of those which I lost as a legislator were later won when I became governor.

For instance, as a state senator I resented the "special deal" pay bills for state department heads. It often seemed that the more political a department head, and the more willing that department head was to walk the halls in the state capitol and buttonhole legislators, the more likely it was that he would receive a pay boost. I resented it. It often meant the more competent, professional department heads, those reluctant to indulge in such politics, got left behind.

While in the state senate, I pushed for some uniform method —for instance, a state salary commission of solid objective credentials to review periodically the top state salaries and make binding recommendations—to improve this situation. I lost that battle while in the legislature, but did win it later while governor.

As was the case in many states, a hodgepodge of education laws had evolved over the years, and this situation had been aggravated by the futile attempts to contrive laws which would circumvent the federal court rulings on racial integration. As a longtime member of our county school board, I had become familiar with school problems and served on a special study commission to draft and implement an omnibus law establishing an updated minimum foundation program for education in our state. This was a first major step toward providing uniform tax assessments and educational opportunities for all children in Georgia.

I was one of only two state legislators on that special education commission. I came to know another member of that commission, a black educator, Dr. Horace Tate, at that time executive director of the black state teachers' organization (later associate director of the integrated Georgia teachers' group and an elected member of the state senate in 1974). He became one of my early supporters when I ran for state office.

I also served on the appropriations committee, and was appalled to discover that we spent all of our time assessing proposals to finance new programs only. Once a program had been in operation for a year, there was little likelihood that it would ever be closely examined again. It would just grow inexorably like a fungus, slowly absorbing for itself larger and larger responsibilities and budgets. Most study commissions not only perpetuated themselves in existence, but often recommended the creation of a new agency of government to deal with newly detected problems. Also, the time spent on a budget item was often inversely proportional to the size of the appropriation. A twenty thousand dollar expenditure for the arts would be scrutinized and criticized from every possible perspective because it was easy to understand. A multi-million-dollar proposal in the university or highway system would be passed perfunctorily because it was complicated and no one took the time to study it.

Another frightening experience was our attempt to write a new constitution for the state. We met in special session in the summer of 1964 and worked industriously to evolve a model document as the fundamental organic law of Georgia. The first shock was when we could not pass the basic bill of rights, guaranteeing freedom from search and freedom of religion. A requirement that God be worshiped was passed by the senate, and a few years later my vote against this requirement, and for the U.S. Constitution language, was used against me as "proof" that I was an atheist! The second shock came when the special interests completed their work on the "simple amendments." In the obscure and obtusely worded paragraphs of the document, a word or two was added here and there for future benefit in lawsuits, tax measures, and utility rate determinations.

It is difficult for the common good to prevail against the intense concentration of those who have a special interest, especially if the decisions are made behind locked doors. What occurred was not illegal, but it was wrong. The 259 members of the legislature were almost all good honest men and women. A tiny portion were not good or honest. In the absence of clear and comprehensive issues, it is simply not possible to marshall the interest of the general public, and under such circumstances legislators often respond to the quiet and professional pressure of lobbyists.

I had time during my four years in the Georgia State Senate to look carefully at how many processes of government work—and to reflect on such matters. Too often the average citizen's real interests become sidetracked for a variety of reasons.

These tremendous pressures on lawmakers who deal with such subjects as taxation or zoning prevent the realization of fairness. Regulatory bodies too often become oriented toward those who are supposed to be regulated, because of their political influence magnified by the relative intensity of their interest in the decisions made. The criminal justice system touches much more heavily the poor than the rich.

There are some interesting inverse relationships in government or societal service which provide a genuine challenge to those who serve in leadership roles. Those who make decisions in our government are most often relatively isolated from the citizens most affected by the decisions. This is especially true in the realm of social services. The hungry, illiterate, unemployed, mentally afflicted, aged, imprisoned, or transient person is rarely interested in the mechanism of government, and under the best of circumstances has very little influence over those who make decisions. Even the most compassionate business or political leader is often prevented by his natural experience from understanding the particular problems of those most needy for whom he is concerned.

The effectiveness of a government bureau responsible for social programs has dramatically different import for public officials and for the recipients of services. How many members of a state legislature or of Congress feel within their own family membership any direct effects of the welfare system, job training programs, prison reform efforts, drug or alcohol rehabilitation centers, unemployment compensation programs, or the public mental and physical health institution? Very few indeed. They can even afford to avoid the public school system if they choose, by sending their children to the more elite and isolated private schools. To poor or afflicted citizens, the public programs mentioned above are crucial factors in their lives.

The poorest families are most often those who are cheated out of what they have. Their options are narrowed down, so they are most compelled to borrow money or to purchase goods from within a small group of suppliers who, sometimes illegitimately, compensate for the higher risks among their customers by charging the highest prices for their money or goods. The honest customer who pays bills on time must also pay for the dishonest or indolent ones who do not pay. Once in debt, or even with the prospect of debt, a timid customer knows the importance of establishing a personal and permanent relationship with one small loan company or with a single local grocer. With the element of competition absent, prices stay up. The entire situation is obviously compounded in seriousness by the lack of mobility and by ignorance or even illiteracy.

Also, the incidence of illness or other affliction falls most heavily on the poor. A study of the most severe cripplers and killers of Georgia people showed clearly that because of a lack of money to pay for health care, a lack of incentive to seek preventive care, and a lack of doctors in their neighborhood, the people in communities with low income suffered most from common, serious physical ailments. Most of the crippling afflictions are preventable if detected and treated early. The range between the highest incidence in any county and the lowest in the healthier counties was dramatic. Of course, the difference—if only the poorer families within a county were considered—would be even more pronounced. Cancer of the breast and cervix, tuberculosis, stroke, venereal disease, and other preventable or curable afflictions varied by a factor as high as twenty to one from one group of citizens to another.

It is obvious that almost inherently the weak, poor, inarticulate, and illiterate citizens feel most severely the consequences of society's ills, and thus contribute to the perpetuation and even aggravation of the problems faced by us all.

Private or governmental efforts to insure justice, good health, enjoyment of life, and maximum enhancement and use of our people's talents are a major concern of our social, religious, professional, and government leaders.

But it requires a conscious and sustained effort to bridge the gap between those who make decisions and the average families who are most directly affected by those decisions. Few leaders make this kind of sustained effort because it is so easy to do otherwise, but it is a necessary ingredient of effective government.

Secrecy is an increasingly pervasive aspect of our governmental process, and with only one or two exceptions is unnecessary and counterproductive. Leaders who deliberately hide their actions from the people rarely do so with benevolent motives. A liar, a cheat, or an incompetent is obviously not going to be eager to have a spotlight focused on evidence of these characteristics. The most ineffective government agency is inherently the one most interested in concealing its performance from the public. If an effective and constructive job is being done, publicity is to be sought. Otherwise, performance and even actual existence is concealed, if possible.

Organizational confusion aggravates government inefficiency and insensitivity. In a disorganized bureaucracy there is no way to fix responsibility, to assess performance, to evolve standard policies, or to establish specific goals. There is almost an automatic perpetuation of failure at an ever-increasing cost. Government withdraws further from its people.

The lobbyists who fill the halls of Congress, state capitols, county courthouses, and city halls often represent well-meaning and admirable groups. They are employees of school teachers, lawyers, doctors, labor union members, bankers, and businessmen. What is often forgotten, however, is that lobbyists seldom represent the average citizen and often express the most selfish aspect of the character of their clients.

Physicians are compassionate and dedicated in alleviating the afflictions of their patients. School teachers serve their students in a self-sacrificial way, and lawyers are genuinely interested in the welfare of their clients. Our businessmen and bankers want to do a good job in serving their customers. But the lobbyists of the medical associations do not even profess to represent the best interests of medical patients; they represent what is best for medical doctors. The lobbyists who represent teachers work for what is best for their own employers. They would not try to cut teachers' salaries or retirement benefits in order to finance a new kindergarten program. Chambers of commerce hire representatives to lobby for their business members and not for the customers of the businesses.

It is hard to imagine lobbyists seeking lower interest payments and less abusive collection procedures if they work for bankers or small-loan organizations.

There is nothing illegal or immoral about all of this. But it must be recognized for what it is.

The elected official, then, is often the only effective representative and voice for the unorganized citizen, the legal client, the medical patient, the student, the borrower of money, or the purchaser of goods. Many officials feel this responsibility constantly and heavily. Others do not.

There are obviously some aspects of our political system which tend to bridge the chasm between political leaders and their constituents. A political campaign itself is both a humbling and truly educational experience. An apparent unconcern or an inadvertently callous statement by a candidate will alienate large numbers of voters.

During a hotly contested election, a fervent effort to understand the issues is imperative for a successful campaigner. This incentive quickly wanes for a secure incumbent who tends to become more and more dependent on those representatives of groups who mount letter-writing campaigns or who visit his office. These entrenched politicians are the very ones who most often occupy the public positions of most seniority and influence. They are also the ones most inclined toward maintaining a high degree of secrecy and a minimum amount of bureaucratic structural simplicity.

Reinhold Niebuhr observes that "The sad duty of politics is to establish justice in a sinful world." He goes on to explain that there is no way to establish or maintain justice without law, that the laws are constantly changing to stabilize the social balance of the competing forces of a dynamic society, and that the sum total of the law is an expression of the structure of government.

Our own basic law, as expressed in historic documents and in court decisions, does represent a striving for justice and fairness, but the practical result often falls far short of our hopes and expectations.

NINE

Running for Governor

The South has been historically Democratic. Even though presidential candidates adopted platforms not popular in our region, as did Al Smith in 1928, our voters never failed to support the Democratic ticket for more than a hundred years. In a heavily Protestant South, and with most of the black voters supporting Nixon, an Irish Catholic from Massachusetts, John F. Kennedy, won a resounding victory in Georgia in 1960.

Four years later, in 1964, it was a different proposition entirely. Vast social and civil-rights programs had been passed by Congress and President Lyndon Johnson; the supporters of Barry Goldwater took full advantage of the disaffection among Georgia voters and waged the best-organized presidential campaign in our state's history. In the process, the Republican Party became viable in my state for the first time in a century. If Barry Goldwater proved a GOP election disaster in most of the country, he still carried Georgia and other Southern states, and ran far better in the South than in the rest of the country.

One of the young leaders among the resurgent Republicans was Howard "Bo" Callaway, a wealthy textile heir, who ran for Congress in my home district in southwest Georgia. His Democratic opponent in 1964 was Garland Byrd, a former lieutenant governor of Georgia and a friend of mine. Unfortunately for him, Garland could never decide whether or not to announce

his public support for President Johnson, and he therefore alien-
ated a number of loyal Democrats, plus losing all of the anti-
Johnson voters to Callaway.

It was a bad time for Democrats in southwest Georgia. My
mother ran Johnson's headquarters in our county seat and frequently had her automobile smeared with soap and her radio
antenna tied in a knot. My son Chip, who was fourteen years old,
has always been interested in politics and proudly wore a campaign
button to school on his shirt. He came home twice with his shirt
pocket torn off, but persisted until one day when some of the big
boys pulled his chair out from under him and roughed him up
rather badly as he lay on the classroom floor. He went out to the
edge of the schoolyard, hid in some bushes, and finally removed
the Democratic Party button. When we came home from work
that night he was crying, more from having removed the button
than from the abuse at school.

In 1964 Goldwater carried Georgia in solid fashion, and
Callaway was elected to Congress. I began then to make quiet
plans to run for Congress in 1966, in spite of the enormous popu-
larity of our new representative. Because he was the first Republican congressman since the War between the States and was
vocal on ideological issues, Callaway was the subject of daily
statewide news coverage. He was the actual leader of his party in
Georgia, and there was considerable conjecture about his being a
future candidate for governor or U.S. senator.

When the legislature adjourned in the spring of 1966, I immediately announced as a candidate for Congress and began a concerted grassroots campaign. Every day I would spend several hours
out in the district, meeting as many people as I could, making a
speech or two, and learning what issues might be of most interest
to the voters. Each night I brought back home a list of names and
addresses. Rosalynn, my sister Gloria, and I laboriously typed an
individualized note to each person. We were making good progress
with this campaign, I thought, though Callaway was still a heavy
favorite.

Then the leading Democratic candidate for governor had a
slight heart attack and withdrew from the race, and our GOP

congressman announced for governor. This apparently left me with a clear shot at the congressional seat, and a poll showed that Callaway was an overwhelming favorite for governor.

I went to Atlanta and attempted to induce two popular state officials to enter the race for governor, but they both decided to wait for a more propitious time.

Many Democrats were ready at that point to concede the governor's office to the Republicans, but many others were not. Some of my fellow state senators, a few women leaders active in statewide civic organizations, and a relatively large group of young people asked me to run for governor. At first I refused. For a few days Senator Herman Talmadge let it be known that he was seriously considering coming back to Georgia to run for governor, but he soon had second thoughts and decided to stay in Washington.

My young friends and I had long discussions about strategy and the rapidly changing political situation in Georgia. Some of them were convinced that I was the only one who was both willing, and perhaps able, to stop Callaway. We drew up voter analyses and prepared tentative budgets. A news story slipped out, and a few more adults became interested and also urged me to run for governor.

It was a tough decision for me to make. It was only three months until the statewide primary, and I was almost completely unknown in the state. We felt that the congressional seat was now mine, and Callaway seemed invulnerable, even to Democrats. Regardless, I decided to run for governor.

I was in my senatorial district at Fort Benning observing a demonstration parachute jump when I had to make a decision. I was called to a field telephone hanging on the side of a tree, and my friends in Atlanta promised me financial support (which never came) and all-out political support (which they delivered). I told them I would go to Plains to talk to Rosalynn, and we agreed on the decision. Then I headed for Atlanta to make final plans for the announcement.

In retrospect, it is difficult to assess all my reasons. Although it is not especially admirable, one of the major reasons was a natural competitiveness with Bo Callaway. He had graduated from West Point just about the same time I completed my work at Annapolis.

When I was a state senator, one of my major projects was to secure a four-year college in southwest Georgia. As a member of the University System Board of Regents, Callaway tried unsuccessfully to block the college. He was leader of the Young Republicans, and in some ways I had become the leader among Georgia's Young Democrats. When we were around each other, both of us were somewhat tense. (Several years later, as governor, I was among those recommending him for appointment as secretary of the army under President Nixon.)

In any case, my family and I began an intensive and frantic campaign around Georgia. We began with almost nonexistent support in much of the state. I was so unknown that some journalists labeled me "Jimmy Who?" Even the many friends in my own congressional district were angry at me for having withdrawn from that campaign after they had given me their early assistance. We called all of our supporters to meet in Atlanta on a Sunday afternoon, and only a handful showed up. Yet we continued this Sunday meeting practice each week, and the number slowly grew. Rosalynn, I, my mother, and my sons campaigned in different directions, and made steady progress.

On Democratic primary election night my supporters and I thought we were in the runoff; and if so would have won. Out of a million or so votes, we finally lost by about twenty thousand.

Former Governor Ellis Arnall and segregationist restaurant owner Lester Maddox came in first and second. The Republicans crossed over in large numbers and supported Maddox in the runoff, thinking that he would be the easier candidate for Callaway to defeat in the general election. Maddox won the nomination.

In the general election in November, Callaway came in first, Maddox second, and Arnall came in third as a write-in candidate. None of them received a majority. An anachronistic Georgia law (changed after that) authorized the state legislature to choose between the first two candidates, and they chose Maddox.

This entire experience was extremely disappointing to me. I was deeply in debt, had lost twenty-two pounds (down to 130), and wound up with Lester Maddox as governor of Georgia.

I waited about one month and then began campaigning again for governor. I remembered the admonition, "You show me a good loser, and I will show you a loser." I did not intend to lose again.

From 1966 through 1970, I worked with more concentration and commitment than ever before in my life. I tried to expand my interests in as many different directions as possible, to develop my own seed business into a profitable and stable enterprise, and to evolve a carefully considered political strategy to win the governor's race in 1970.

I helped to organize an eight-county planning and development commission, and served for several years as its chairman. I studied the techniques of long-range planning as it related to regional development. We tried to assess what our rural counties and people possessed in natural and human resources, what we would like to be in years to come, and the alternative courses of action open to us. We learned as planners to assume the roles of servants and not masters, and we also learned to combine practical implementation plans with theoretical concepts of planning.

A small group of us later decided to organize a statewide planning society, primarily to correlate the experiences we had had within the regional planning commissions, colleges, and private businesses—all devoted to planning and development. I was elected the first state president, and we began to discuss how the business and professional communities might join with government in a more cooperative approach to make services more beneficial to our people. We talked about government organization, budget priorities, economic development, recreation and tourism, transportation, health, and social justice.

I stayed active in professional seed organizations and also became state chairman of the March of Dimes. Our only civic club in Plains was Lions International, and I had been a member of the club since the first week I came back home from the navy. This was one of the most gratifying opportunities for service. There are about 180 Lions clubs in Georgia, and in many small towns they are the focal point for almost all public activity. I was elected district governor and then chairman of the six regional district governors in Georgia.

My church life became far more meaningful to me, and every year I went with other laymen on pioneer mission trips to other states or to special areas in Georgia.

My brother, Billy, had come back home to work with me in our business, and it became a complete family effort, with our families —mine and Billy's—working together.

On a typical day I would go to the warehouse or farm early and perform my extracurricular duties, along with my regular business work, until late in the afternoon. Then I would drive somewhere in Georgia to make a speech, and return home late at night. Names, information about the community, and speech notes for later use were all dictated into a small tape recorder in the automobile. The next day Rosalynn wrote thank-you notes on an automatic typewriter which also recorded names, addresses, and code descriptions of the persons I had met.

At other times I studied issues and prepared speech notes on subjects relating to state government. I wrote my own speeches, sometimes spending several days and reading three or four books to prepare an original one on environment, or health, crime control or criminal justice, or certain aspects of education. All of this was an enjoyable and ultimately fruitful experience.

We had a superb group of young volunteer workers who helped me with the analysis of issues, the preparation of a future campaign platform, and the detailed study of all voting results since 1952. For each of the 159 Georgia counties we prepared colored charts and graphs showing how the people there had voted in state and federal elections for all different kinds of candidates, emphasizing all kinds of issues. Since we knew the candidates and issues, it was instructive for us to compare the relative strengths of the candidates from one election to another. After a little study, the general impression of voter motivations in the individual counties began to form.

The overwhelming favorite in the 1970 governor's election was former Governor Carl Sanders, although many other candidates were also mentioned, and several entered the campaign. With the exception of my family and a few close workers, almost all of my best friends advised me not to run for governor. Most of them advocated a campaign for lieutenant governor, and some thought that I should run for commissioner of agriculture. There was never the slightest hesitancy on my part about what to do. I thought I could run and win, and I never worried at all about who else might be in the race against me.

As the election approached, I stepped up the pace of the campaign and ultimately made about eighteen hundred speeches during the four-year campaign. Rosalynn and I in that time personally shook hands with more than six hundred thousand people in Georgia—more than half the total number who vote. During the last few months each of us would meet at least three factory shifts each day.

We shook hands with entire crowds who came to high-school football games, livestock and tobacco sale barns, rodeos, college athletic events, and horse shows. Between these we would visit

The Carter handshake carried him to the state senate and governorship—Jimmy and Rosalynn shook hands with 600,000 Georgians in the 1970 campaign.

every barber shop, beauty parlor, restaurant, store, and service station in a town, and then move on to the next one. We stood for hours in front of swinging doors at major shopping centers, meeting every customer who entered the most heavily patronized business places. When it was too early in the morning for people to be at work, we met them at downtown bus terminals, or went to the assembly points for municipal policemen, firemen, maintenance crews, or garbage collectors.

In every instance, one or two of our local volunteer workers would be with us, having scouted the locations to determine the most effective way to utilize our scarce time. To each person we met we gave an excellent little threefold pamphlet, which was edited and illustrated well enough that it would be kept and read. We learned about scheduling, living off the land, and using maximum free news media coverage to supplement good paid advertising. Rosalynn and I seldom went together, but would sometimes meet for major events too large to handle alone.

Neither we nor our staff workers stayed in hotels or motels for which we had to pay. We lived with supporters all over the state, and the late-night visits helped more than anything else to cement permanent friendships—and to let an effective exchange of information take place between campaign headquarters and people in the individual communities of Georgia. We personally visited the isolated country radio stations, many of which had to operate with a staff of only one or two persons. When we showed up at the station, they almost always welcomed a live or taped interview.

Those small radio stations often put you close to the people. I remember months later, after becoming governor and after having signed into law a "Sunshine" bill opening legislative and executive department meetings to the public, I was being interviewed on one of the country stations. Complaining about the new law, a farmer called in to say, "My papa always told me there were two things which nobody should ever see being made. One is potted meat, and the other is laws!"

My chief opponent in the 1970 campaign got almost all of the endorsements—from newspapers, judges, sheriffs, legislators, bankers, lawyers, and organized groups of all types. We made an issue of the big shots standing between him and the people, and eventually almost every endorsement (which he avidly sought) cost him votes in some fashion or other.

We had several serious setbacks and made some bad mistakes. Money was always a problem. We set a quota for the primary of fifteen cents for every person in the state. If campaign workers volunteered to help, we asked how big an area they would cover. Then we computed the population of the area, multiplied by fifteen cents, and assigned that as a fund-raising quota to the worker. In a few areas it worked. We eventually raised about half this primary amount for all three campaigns combined—the primary, runoff, and general election. We often just cut back our budget when money was scarce, recruited more volunteers, and worked harder.

My biggest problem and worst mistake involved one of the Atlanta newspapers. The editor early in the campaign began to characterize me as an ignorant and bigoted redneck peanut farmer. Editorial cartoons showed me standing in the muck of racism while all the other candidates disappeared into the sunrise of

Jimmy Carter was inaugurated as Georgia's seventy-sixth governor in January 1971.

enlightenment. These attacks had a serious effect on some of our tentatively committed, liberal, and idealistic supporters who did not know me personally, particularly those in the Atlanta area who might have helped us financially. Since the newspaper strongly supported former Governor Sanders, I presume that the editors had recognized me as his major potential opponent and wanted to destroy me early in the campaign. The attack actually backfired, because it projected me into a position of prominence among the many candidates in the race.

I wrote an ill-tempered letter attacking the newspaper, but it was not published. When all the candidates were invited to address the annual convention of the Georgia Press Association, I used my time on the program to read the letter to all the state's editors. It was a mistaken and counterproductive action.

This altercation also hurt me among the black voters in the primary. Throughout the campaign I had established a standard practice of working among them on an equal basis with whites. I was the only candidate who visited all the communities in cities, and who spent a large part of my time within the predominantly black stores, restaurants, and street areas. Although I did poorly among black citizens in the Democratic primary, I did well in the general election.

With a last-minute surge, we won the election handily.

TEN

Governor

Once while I was campaigning for governor, I went into a school-house in Columbus to meet with some black teachers and administrative officers who were influential among the voters of the neighborhood. I introduced myself to the group and walked around the room shaking hands with the people there. All of them told me somewhat proudly who they were and what their positions were.

The last was a much younger person, whom I later learned was a teacher's aide. She did not offer to meet me, and when I approached her she seemed to be timid and embarrassed. I repeated my name and asked, "What is your name?" After a few moments, she blurted out sincerely, "I ain't nobody!" Everyone laughed, except me and the young woman. When my brief visit was over, I asked if I might talk to her, and in an ineffective way tried to explain that she was certainly important to me and that she was one of the primary reasons I was running for office. I am not sure that she ever understood what I was trying to say.

One other incident comes to mind. In 1970, as the long campaign was drawing to a close, people began to see in me their probable next state executive officer. As I stood during early-morning hours in factory shift lines or later in the day in front of revolving doors at shopping-center stores, many people would stop to speak a few words, and quite often the words were obviously heartfelt and important. Frequently there was a statement concerning mentally retarded children who were either at home or receiving inadequate care at the state's hospitals. I was emphasizing more and more in my public statements the problems of Georgia's mental health program, but did not actually have a definitive program prepared for implementation when I became governor. My seriousness about the subject and my awareness of my future responsibilities both were increased substantially when a man approached me one day in a supermarket where I was shaking hands with the customers. He said he was working for me, and I thanked him. I started to turn away, and he asked, "Do you know why?" I shook my head, and he said simply, "Because I have a retarded baby."

I thought about episodes like these when I wrote my eight-minute inauguration speech, in part of which I stated:

> . . . Our people are our most precious possession. We cannot afford to waste the talents and abilities given by God to one single person. . . . Every adult illiterate, every school drop-out, and every untrained retarded child is an indictment of us all. Our state pays a terrible and continuing human and financial price for these failures. It is time to end this waste. If Switzerland and Israel and other people can eliminate illiteracy, then so can we.
>
> At the end of a long campaign, I believe I know the people of this state as well as anyone. Based on this knowledge of Georgians north and south, rural and urban, liberal and conservative, I say to you quite frankly that the time for racial discrimination is over. Our people have already made this major and difficult decision, but we cannot underestimate the challenge of hundreds of minor decisions yet to be made. Our inherent human charity and our religious beliefs will be taxed to the limit. No poor, rural, weak, or black person should ever have to bear the additional burden of being deprived of the opportunity of an education, a job, or simple justice.

All parts of the country have been struggling with these kinds of challenges, but perhaps in the South the struggles have been most difficult, and sometimes most newsworthy. After I was elected governor, and other new governors like Reubin Askew, Dale Bumpers, and John West were elected in Florida, Arkansas, and South Carolina, there was a rash of articles written about the "New South." Reporters came to see us, from all over the nation and from many foreign countries. Yet there was often an insinuation that somehow a few progressive candidates had misled the Southern voters and had captured the governors' offices by subterfuge. Nothing could be further from the truth. As accurately as possible, we represented the people who had elected us. The "major and difficult decisions" had already been made.

Now it was time for the challenge of the "hundreds of minor decisions," and they surrounded me during four years as governor. We were lucky not to have any major racial conflagrations during my term, but there were still many actions to be taken during those years following the end of legal segregation in the South.

During the years before I was elected, massive efforts had to be mounted by the Georgia State Patrol to maintain order in the communities of our state; threats of racial disturbance arose and were assuaged by demonstrations of uniformed force. From 1968 through 1970, just before I took office, the number of man-hours of uniformed patrolmen's time spent on civil disorders per year rose from 12,113 to 45,910. Instead of using state patrolmen to such an extent, we formed a biracial civil-disorder unit (CDU). It consisted of three persons, and we trained them to go into a community when any threat to peace was detected. This crew, dressed in civilian clothes, entered a community quietly, used a maximum of communication and persuasion, a minimum of publicity, and no force. By 1973 only 177 man-hours of our state patrol officers' time were spent in civil-disorder work. In the aftermath of any potential racial disturbance, there was often left a permanent local organization or committee to assure continuing communications between black and white leaders in a community. Because of their success, our CDU members were asked to visit several other states to explain their methods of operation.

It was obvious, too, in my state that drastic penal reform was needed, and every effort was made to analyze the basis of the problems in our state's prisons. I persuaded Ellis MacDougall, head of the prison system in Connecticut, to come South again. MacDougall, a professional criminologist, had spent eighteen years in the South Carolina prison system and had earned a national reputation as director of corrections in that state. He had gone to Connecticut two-and-one-half years before to head and improve that state's prison system. He seemed delighted to come back South to work at improving Georgia's prison system with the full backing of my administration.

I remember thinking that, second only to governmental reorganization, improving the criminal justice system in my state could be my greatest contribution as governor.

This proved to be a very difficult subject, and in the prison system no overall reduction was ever realized in the number of inmates in our institutions. But prison educational programs were multiplied fourfold, treatment programs increased 150 percent, and the number of professional counselors more than quadrupled. In 1971 no warden held a college degree, but within three years more than half had bachelor's degrees, and several held more advanced degrees.

It was my privilege as governor to appoint dozens of qualified black citizens to major policy board positions, so they could participate fully in official deliberations such as those concerning the university system, the corrections system, state law enforcement, all aspects of human resources, the pardon and parole system, and the professional examination boards for dentists, physicians, nurses, funeral directors, beauticians and barbers, and many more.

One appointment which was particularly well received involved state senator Horace Ward. When he accepted his appointment to a judgeship, he quietly pointed out that he had tried unsuccessfully to enter the Georgia Law School several years ago, but had been denied admittance because he was black. Although his lawsuit for admission was ultimately successful, he had already completed law school outside the state before the decision was final.

There were thousands of schoolchildren each week visiting the state capitol building to learn about our history and our government. Portraits of famous Georgians—governors, senators, poets, authors, editors, industrialists, educators, and founders of national organizations—almost cover the walls of the building. Every single portrait was of a white citizen, though it seemed obvious that many black leaders had played major roles in the shaping of our state's society. As both a substantive and symbolic gesture, I decided to select several notable black citizens and honor them by hanging their portraits in the state capitol. At the first meeting of the selection committee there was an immediate and unanimous decision that Nobel Laureate Martin Luther King, Jr. should be included, and a thorough assessment procedure was devised to select the others.

This was a proper and long-overdue action, and it received approval from the vast majority of our people. But there were a few vocal dissenters. Lester Maddox announced that when he was elected governor to succeed me that the King portrait would be instantly removed. (He was soundly trounced in the 1974 election.)

On the Sunday afternoon of February 17, 1974, a small band of Ku Klux Klansmen straggled around outside the capitol while the portrait of the black civil-rights leader was unveiled. The capitol was packed as Secretary of State Ben Fortson recounted the accomplishments of Dr. King.

Fortson, a white-haired veteran of many years in the state capitol, has long been a glorious speaker to groups of schoolchildren visiting the capitol, talking to them of American history and American ideals. That day he was eloquent in talking about Dr. King and the meaning of his life, especially for black Americans, and in the end Fortson led the white and black audience in singing the anthem of so many civil-rights marches, "We Shall Overcome."

The two other black Georgians whose portraits were unveiled that day were Lucy Laney and Bishop Henry McNeal Turner, both influential nineteenth-century figures.

This was a small gesture in a way, the hanging of these portraits, but it seemed especially significant to those who had assembled for the ceremony. It seemed to me that everyone was aware of how far we had come during the last few years, but were much more cognizant of how far we had to go. There was a dramatization of the goodwill that has long existed between the black and white people of our state, and the realization that no matter what the future holds we must face it together.

A new degree of freedom for both black and white Southerners evolved from the trauma of desegregation. Instead of constant preoccupation with the racial aspect of almost every question, public officials, black and white, are now at liberty to make objective decisions about education, health, employment, crime control, consumer protection, prison reform, and environmental quality.

Outside of the metropolitan areas, integration of the public school systems is complete because of the historic intermixing of white and black homes. As described earlier, on farms and in small towns there has always been a close personal relationship between individual black and white citizens, even when the strictest legal segregation was observed in public facilities and at social functions. After *de jure* segregation ended, there was no need to walk across the street and say, "I would like to introduce myself. I'm your white neighbor who has lived here for the last forty years."

Living in the same neighborhoods and working on the same jobs often created a personal and individual basis of mutual understanding and respect. To an amazing degree the lives of both black and white Southerners have been centered around the church. The "Bible Belt" designation is substantiated in fact. A burgeoning economy with relatively low unemployment rates—at least in the 1960s and early 1970s—attenuated what could have been a continuing and bitter racial struggle for scarce jobs. Biracial high-school athletic teams were first feared and then accepted within the confines of community pride.

These factors have been among those which prevented the terrible racial clashes, feared by many in the South when integration seemed inevitable.

ELEVEN

Start From Zero

As a new governor I found the problems, authority, and opportunities to be greater than I had anticipated.

I enjoyed my four years in this office, in spite of its being a highly controversial, aggressive, and combative administration. I habitually arrived at the capitol no later than 7:15 A.M. and never awakened in the early morning without looking forward to the day with pleasant anticipation. The long-range planning, detailed administration, study and preparation of legislative proposals, legislative struggles, visits with Georgians of all kinds, press conferences, major speeches, analyses of federal/state interrelationships, and other similar duties were all components of a challenging and enjoyable experience.

At first I was surprised at the disorganization of the governmental processes. Following the election, I began to prepare the budget for the coming year. Piled on a table were departmental funding requests that amounted to more than half again as much money as would be available. No one had made any attempt to assess the worth of the requests or to arrange them in any sort of priority. I worked with my budget staff every night for six weeks on this confusing mess, and I became more convinced than ever that my own developing concepts of what I called "zero-base budgeting" were necessary.

As was the case with almost every government, the only analyses of funding requests were those for new or expanded programs. No method existed for the analysis on an equal basis for old and

The Governor of Georgia, in his office

perhaps obsolete programs which had been ensconced within the governmental bureaucracy years ago. The cost of new programs consisted of just a small portion of total expenditures. Once a bureaucratic entity had been established, it was almost immune from later scrutiny. Often these agencies would either grow like cancers or retreat into self-perpetuating obscurity.

We changed all of this in my state and devised a procedure whereby the future budgets would start from scratch—at zero! It meant chopping the state government up into individual functions and analyzing each service delivery system annually, regardless of whether it was fifty years old or a brand-new proposal for a future program. The analyses were done on a one-page form by the person deep within the department responsible for performing the service. Each of these forms was called a "decision package," and within each department they were arranged in a descending order of priority. Several discussions with the head of the department were usually necessary before I would accept the priority arrangements.

Each decision package was assigned a computer code number to describe the kind of service being delivered, which later made it automatic to detect duplications when the numbers were printed out sequentially by the computer. To offer just two examples, we identified seven agencies responsible for the education of deaf children, and twenty-two responsible for the utilization of water resources.

I had run on a platform promising reorganization of the state government, stating that there were 146 agencies in all. Our later analysis revealed 300, and we abolished 278 of them! Every major department had its own independent computer system. We created just one central system. Each large or small agency had its own printing system. We merged forty-three of them into one system. No merit-system employees were discharged because of government reorganization—that was a personal pledge of mine—but we filled only a portion of the vacancies when they occurred through normal attrition.

We found innovative ways to save money. For instance, the board of regents of the university system traveled more than the Georgia State Patrol. In many cities around the state there would be three, four, and sometimes five radio repair shops for different departments of state government, each one overstaffed and underworked, sometimes in adjacent buildings. Some departments of state government responded very enthusiastically to the chance for improving themselves. We amended the Georgia Constitution to permit the payment of incentive awards amounting to 10 percent of the savings for the first year. One suggestion was that the state cease mowing down into the ditches and up on the off-shore banks all the way out to the highway right-of-way, but instead mow only thirty feet from the center line of the right-hand lane of the road. This permitted the flourishing of Georgia wildflowers, bushes, and trees as things of beauty along our highways. It cut down drastically on the cost and danger of mowing steep banks. It enhanced the retention of soil on the right-of-way slopes and will ultimately result in the concealing of unsightly billboards. In addition to this, the cost of highway maintenance was reduced about 15 percent for the whole state.

Another improvement that occurred in the transportation department was the analysis of what engineers did in the supervision of highway contract fulfillment on construction of roads. We had engineers measuring and weighing all the ingredients that went into road plant mix, others who manned public scales to weigh the dump trucks full and empty as they carried the plant mix to the construction site, another supervising the dumping of asphalt mix on the road, the compaction of it with machines (they measured the thickness of it as it was done and then later certified that the job had been done properly). We changed all this to end-result inspection whereby all these men were replaced with one person who went along periodically as short sections of the highway were completed, made test borings, and sent the samples to the laboratory where they were analyzed for content and thickness. Thereby, we not only saved tremendous personnel requirements, but let engineers again do what they were trained to do in supervising proper highway construction.

At enormous expense to the taxpayers, Georgia state patrolmen were being trained, uniformed, and provided with an automobile. Yet quite often these men were then assigned to patrol-station duties of typing up accident report forms and manning the radios. As a result of another suggestion, we moved almost one hundred of these troopers out to patrol the highways and replaced them with handicapped Georgians who had been trained by vocational rehabilitation as professional typists, and we trained them as professional radio operators. The many benefits are obvious.

In the multitude of departments that existed prior to the formation of the Human Resources Department, we sometimes had five or six different caseworkers going into one home and maintaining five or six different files on the same family. This was causing an enormous waste of manpower and an ineffective administration of human services—because there was no personal involvement between the caseworkers and the family. When we merged mental and physical health, retardation, vocational rehabilitation, welfare, alcoholism, drugs, problems of the aged, and juvenile offenders into one department, we could have one or, at the most, two caseworkers serving a particular family with different kinds of afflictions.

Naturally, there was intense opposition from the bureaucrats who thrived on confusion, from special interests who preferred to work in the dark, and from a few legislative leaders who did not want to see their fiefdoms endangered. But the people insisted on the changes, and they were made.

Preceding this reorganization process, during the first months of my term, we had fifty-one public meetings around the state, attended by thousands of Georgians, to formulate specific long-range goals in every realm of public life. We spelled out in writing what we hoped to accomplish at the end of two, five, or even twenty years in the fields of mental and physical health, tax equalization, education, prison reform, transportation, criminal justice, preservation of historic sites and natural areas, environmental quality, and industrial development. Our people were encouraged to express their criticisms and suggestions and to describe how their most important needs could be met.

One of the gratifying aspects of the administration was the remarkable cooperation of the business and professional community. They were eager to see some order brought out of the chaos of government and contributed hundreds of days of hard work during the reorganization effort. They also joined in selling the programs to the legislature and to the general public. None of them ever asked for any special favor or privileged treatment in return.

I cannot overemphasize how often this has been my experience —how many people of integrity and competence are willing to take part in politics and government without anything much to gain personally, without any selfish motive. I found this true in Georgia, and I am finding it true all over the nation.

Some of the changes we made in state government removed special advantages which had been enjoyed for generations by powerful financial interests. For instance, our state keeps on hand at any time more than $300 million in funds which have been collected in taxes and not yet spent. Previously, these funds had been parcelled out to "friendly" banks as political favors, and the taxpayers of Georgia had lost enormous sums in uncollected inter-est. A standard procedure had been to place money in such banks at low interest. Hundreds of other accounts were maintained all over the state, with no interest being paid on them at all. We changed all of this by activating a depository board which con-ducted our business in public, by creating a computer cash flow model to determine the optimum type of investment, and by investing our currently available funds among the state's banks by competitive sealed bids. Interest income increased 244 percent in four years. After a few initial expressions of concern, almost all members of the banking community accepted the new system with gratitude that finally the state's banking business was being con-ducted openly, decently, and free of political intrigue.

All of these changes combined to permit the slashing of the administrative costs of government by more than half and to let us provide substantially improved services without any tax increases.

As a matter of fact, the first year we implemented zero-base budgeting, our supplemental budget change in the middle of the year was a *negative* $53 million, whereas we ordinarily expected an increase of more than $20 million. When I left office our state sur-plus was almost $200 million, and because of an underestimation of savings from reorganization, the fiscal year 1975 budget was actually $10 million lower than the fiscal year 1974 budget had been.

Government at all levels can be competent, economical, and efficient. Yet I would hasten to point out that nowhere in the Constitution of the United States, or the Declaration of Indepen-dence, or the Bill of Rights, or the Emancipation Proclamation, or the Old Testament, or the New Testament do you find the words "economy" or "efficiency." Not that these two words are unim-portant, but you discover other words like *honesty, integrity, fair-ness, liberty, justice, courage, patriotism, compassion, love*—and many others which describe what a human being ought to be. These are also the same words which describe what a government of human beings ought to be.

TWELVE

Government and the Outdoors

With the exception of reorganization itself, I spent more time preserving our natural resources than on any other one issue.

As was the case in many other states, we went through the crisis of working out environmental protection laws while I was governor. We had many cliff-hanging confrontations in passing our total package of new bills.

The problems of state government were constantly aggravated by the haphazard attitude of the administration in Washington. While I was governor, the confusion and unpredictability of the federal government and its agencies created an exasperating and discouraging situation. Programs were started and then aborted, reasonable and omnibus bills were vetoed and subsequently passed over the veto, and then appropriated funds were impounded. The multitude of federal agencies involved defied comprehension, and they often worked at cross-purposes.

Major programs in land use, welfare reform, environmental protection, student loans, transportation, housing, and revenue sharing were proposed with great fanfare. But their original purpose was either subverted or the programs were abandoned altogether. Since our legislature meets briefly only once a year to prepare a budget for eighteen months in the future, this lack of purpose and planning in Washington makes it almost impossible to correlate the efforts of local, state, and federal governments in the delivery of services to our people.

I was the only governor who testified against revenue sharing for the states. *In the first place, there was no revenue to share.* The money was simply stolen from the poor and afflicted people of this nation, who have been served through categorical grant programs, and delivered to state governments for distribution, ideally to be shared by all citizens of the state on an equal basis.

Local governments do desperately need additional funding opportunities. But if there were some coherence in the administration of federal programs, local governments could do a better job with funds they presently have available.

Inevitably, under our present tax laws the income of the federal government increases at a very rapid rate compared to that of state and local governments. For instance, each time the gross national product goes up a certain amount, say 100, state government income goes up almost exactly the same amount. Federal government income goes up 135, local government increases only 72. So over a period of time, there ought to be a shift of funding from the federal government to the local governments because of the regressive and tightly constrained source of local funds which is derived primarily from property tax. Whatever revenue sharing funds are available should go only to local governments, not to states, except perhaps in Alaska and Hawaii where most local services are provided by state funds.

Our early historical sites were originally chosen for settlement because of their favorable locations, and these physical attractions still exist as a lure for modern land developers. Many of them were being rapidly destroyed by bulldozers, and there was no effective means of protecting them. Modern-day owners were under the combined pressures of rising tax levies and minimal production of income. We established and funded the Georgia Heritage Trust, designed to inventory and assess more than two thousand such sites. We acquired many of them while I was governor, and this will be a continuing commitment of our state government.

About thirty other sites of similar importance have been purchased or been given to the state, and the entire process has now been adopted by our people as a valuable public effort.

Some of the sites examined by the Georgia Heritage Trust had unusual histories. Chinese laborers came to Augusta years ago to build a winding canal through the city. They remained to work in textile mills built along the canal. There is now a park of some hundreds of acres, using the canal as a focal point. Their descendants have become outstanding and respected citizens of that community.

Although several altercations arose concerning the protection of valuable places in Georgia during my term in office, the most controversial of all was with the ultimate land developer in wild places, the U.S. Army Corps of Engineers. For years the Corps had made plans to build a major dam on the Flint River as it flowed down the granite slopes of Georgia's fall line fifty miles southeast of Atlanta. Assuming that the reports and computations of the Corps were accurate, almost everyone, including myself, had supported the project. It was to provide apparently much-needed broad-water recreation, generate large amounts of electrical power, control floods, purify the river's water, and provide financial benefits, over a period of a hundred years, which were 160 percent of costs.

It became obvious to me that none of these claims were true. I inspected the site thoroughly by air and traversed the river twice by canoe. Public hearings raised several embarrassing questions, and both Senator Herman Talmadge and I became concerned. Senator Talmadge, a supporter of the project, requested that the General Accounting Office of the Congress substantiate the computations and claims of the Corps of Engineers. I asked the Corps for their detailed analyses and for data to support their claims of benefits, but there was a continuing series of delays in sending me this information. In January of 1973, the "revised" report was promised in April, and then later in June. In August it was finally delivered to me.

The report they delivered was primarily promotional literature supporting the dam construction. Exaggerated claims for benefits were combined with shrunken costs estimated to justify the project. Although the major benefit claimed was for recreation, all state and federal recreation agencies strongly and officially opposed the project, pointing out that there were many underused lakes within a fifty-mile radius of the proposed damsite, including one federally financed lake, only twenty-six miles from the Spewrell Bluff site, going bankrupt because it was not being adequately used! Our state's recent surveys had proved that the type of recreation most in need was open, free-flowing streams, and not broad-water lakes.

Population figures for future years in the area in the Corps' report had been strangely doubled, electrical power generators would have to run at more than 125 percent capacity, and broad mud flats would be exposed when any appreciable power was actually generated. The Corps admitted that the small stream flow would only permit power generation forty-two days each year. Flood control benefits had been increased by a factor of 287 percent since the initial estimates, and it was found that any flood control would result only by lowering the water level in times of potential flooding, which would expose the mud flats and reduce or eliminate power generation and recreation benefits. In just a few months the Corps more than quadrupled the economic benefits from recreation, and federal recreational advantages computed by the Corps were 1,650 percent more than those which had been originally computed by the National Park Service.

The General Accounting Office report confirmed my own computations, but did not make them public until more than a year later. I vetoed the dam project and called on Congress to reassess other similar porkbarrel projects which had been approved for possible construction around the nation.

On one-day or two-day weekend trips, Rosalynn and I visited the beautiful natural areas of our state. We rode the wild rivers on rafts and in canoes and kayaks. We panned successfully for gold in a remote north Georgia stream. We studied the wildlife programs on our isolated game preserves, and inspected the virgin cypress groves on Lewis Island in the mouth of the Altamaha River.

Our favorite place was Cumberland Island, off the southeast Georgia coast, where one can see dozens of sea turtles coming ashore to lay their eggs in the early summer. We would watch the sun rise over the Atlantic and drive down twenty miles of the broad, white beach without seeing another living soul. We observed alligators and pileated woodpeckers and fished for bass in

Jimmy Carter is at home in the outdoors.

the fresh-water lake that is, in all the world, closest to the sea. An hour in a flat boat would produce enough conches, clams, and oysters to last our family for several days, and wild pigs were always available when we developed a taste for barbecue. Some of the northernmost of Georgia's coastal islands still contain the ruins of

European settlements which were established by the Spaniards—almost one hundred years before the first English settlers landed at Jamestown.

On the outskirts of Atlanta, the Chattahoochee River approaches from the northeast, cold and clear. Canoeists and rafters ride its rapids, and fishermen catch brown and rainbow trout within sight of the expressways, office buildings, and housing developments. Muskrats and wood ducks are plentiful. This entire river is threatened by uncontrolled land development and flexible zoning policies. Several key sites along the river have now been acquired by the state and local governments for preservation and limited use, and a comprehensive plan has been developed for the entire forty-two-mile stretch of river above Atlanta. It is a beautiful river. A Georgia poet, Sidney Lanier, wrote of it in "The Song of the Chattahoochee":

> Out of the hills of Habersham,
> Down the valleys of Hall,
> I hurry amain to reach the plain,
> Run the rapid and leap the fall,
> Split at the rock and together again,
> Accept my bed, or narrow or wide,
> And flee from folly on every side
> With a lover's pain to attain the plain
> Far from the hills of Habersham,
> Far from the valleys of Hall.

Sidney Lanier would recognize many of Georgia's beautiful, wild, natural areas today, like the Chattahoochee, as being close to the way he viewed them one hundred years ago. It would be a bitter shame if all this natural beauty were not preserved for our children's children's children to view with joy one hundred years from now.

THIRTEEN

Our International Neighbors

Every concerned American has given thought in recent years to this nation's foreign policy, both its flaws and successes. It has been a field of keen interest to me since my days at Annapolis, when my awareness of American military power helped focus a more general concern on the United States' role in the world.

Recently I met with about a dozen of our nation's top political writers for several hours of discussion about subjects of current interest and major importance. During a heated exchange, one of the reporters exclaimed, "There is no place for morality in foreign policy!" Although he later modified his position, he perhaps inadvertently described the feelings of many Americans about foreign policy as effectuated in recent years.

As it has related to such areas as Pakistan, Chile, Cambodia, and Vietnam, our government's foreign policy has not exemplified any commitment to moral principles. Furthermore, each time we have become embroiled in an embarrassing predicament, it has become apparent that our leaders have often departed from the more honest inclinations of the American people. This has required varying degrees of secrecy and outright lying.

A nation's domestic and foreign policy actions should be derived from the same standards of ethics, honesty, and morality which are characteristic of the individual citizens of the nation. The people of this country are inherently unselfish, open, honest, decent, competent, and compassionate. Our government should be the same, in all its actions and attitudes.

There is only one nation in the world which is capable of true leadership among the community of nations, and that is the United States of America. Many citizens of other countries know this to be true and have looked with concern and consternation on our fumbling and heavy-handed administration of ill-advised international policies during the last few years. During my own travels in the Far East, Europe, the Americas, and the Mideast, I have found a natural friendship toward the American people, but a growing distrust of our government.

As governor, I tried to establish a proper relationship with foreign governments and peoples in spite of the natural limitations of an individual state to conduct foreign affairs. During the last two years of my term, we made personal and official visits to ten other nations. In each instance, our goal was to promote friendship and trade and to learn as much as possible about our hosts. It was gratifying to discover the interest which foreign leaders displayed in having the governor of an American state in their country. We were almost always permitted to prepare our own itinerary and to arrange visits with political, economic, and cultural leaders who could best teach us about their native land.

Atlanta now has a large and rapidly growing consular corps, and our state has opened and maintains full-time trade offices in Brussels, Bonn, Sao Paulo, Toronto, and Tokyo. Plans are now underway to open additional offices in London and in the Middle East.

We have sent repeated delegations of our business leaders to the nations I have visited, in order to follow up on trade opportunities for Georgia products and customers. It soon became obvious that additional centers for international meetings and display of goods were needed in our state, so we decided to build a mammoth World Trade Center in Atlanta for these purposes.

We have a sister state in Brazil named Pernambuco. After Rosalynn and I visited its capital city of Recife in 1972, we helped to arrange for an annual exchange of private citizens between the two states. Each year a planeload of about two hundred Georgians flies to Pernambuco, and a similar number of Pernambucans come to visit us. All of these visitors live for a couple of weeks in private homes and participate in a series of special events designed to teach them about the character and customs of their hosts. This has been an exciting experience for hundreds of our people and has reminded us anew that we share one world where peace and friendship can be a natural part of international life.

In addition to learning about the business and political affairs and becoming acquainted with the leaders of other nations, these visits have been very helpful in understanding international matters of great interest to our own people.

During a recent visit to Germany I had a long conversation with Dr. Helmut Schmidt, who was then Finance Minister and who has since become Chancellor. After discussing the relative costs of labor and production and the desirability for German investments in the United States, he asked me to assess the status of our nation's energy policy. I replied that we did not have one. He was surprised that I would say this and stated that surely all industrialized countries must have carefully considered energy policies. I insisted that we did not and asked him in what form his government's energy policy existed. He replied that for economists and government leaders there was a computer model which contained current data about sources of supply, prices, processing, and consumption. For other less technically oriented people, there was a printed volume of about two hundred pages containing graphs and tables, with a simple explanation of the probable impact of changes in sources of supply or price variations on the German people and markets.

I asked for a copy of the book, and Dr. Schmidt promised to send me a copy when I returned home. After a couple of months, Dr. Schmidt was made Chancellor, and my book had not arrived. I assumed that he had simply forgotten to send it to me. One day the German consul general came in and announced that he had brought me a package from the Chancellor. I smiled and said that I thought he had forgotten. "No," he replied, "the Chancellor sends his apologies for the delay and said that it took him longer than he had anticipated to have a copy translated from German into English." It was an excellent book; we still at this writing have no similar explanation of a comprehensive national energy policy for the United States.

A trip to Israel was carefully arranged to yield maximum

opportunity to learn about the country and to meet with the military and political leaders for intensive briefings. Prime Minister Rabin, Mrs. Meir, and the ministers of foreign affairs, finance, and trade privately discussed with me the problems and opportunities of their nation. The chief of military intelligence described the defense posture of the beleagured country, and we went to sea with the Cherbourg missile boats to learn about naval defense capabilities. We spent several days traveling around Israel, visiting the kibbutzim, the Golan Heights, Jordan's West Bank, and other strategically important places.

One of our most enjoyable experiences was having lunch with the mayor and vice-mayor of Nazareth, and the mayor of New Nazareth. It was an exotic and beautiful meal in the mayor's home overlooking the downtown part of the city. We had not eaten for a full day before arriving there, and we repeatedly cleaned our plates of the roast sheep, candied fruits, and vegetables. Only later did we learn that a host can never permit a guest to leave with a clean plate because it is an indication that the guest was still hungry. I will never forget the coffee, which was the consistency of thick syrup.

The mayor was a Muslim, the vice-mayor a Christian, and the mayor of New Nazareth was a Jew. The latter was then furiously building new apartments for the stream of Russian emigrants who were arriving daily. They were immediately incorporated into the life of their new community. Within two days after leaving Russia the new families were studying Hebrew, the children were in school, and the parents were employed in one of the new factories which were springing up around the growing new city.

In England I was particularly impressed with the interrogation of the cabinet ministers in the House of Commons, and believe that it would be helpful here to have members of the cabinet appear before joint sessions of the Congress to answer written and verbal questions, preferably with live television coverage for the whole nation to view.

Within the Latin American countries we found tremendous personal warmth and also frustration at our relative unconcern with the affairs of our own hemisphere. Our hosts received with amusement and appreciation my attempt to speak Spanish during several dozen press conferences and speeches. After returning home we worked with other Georgia leaders to bring to Atlanta the 1974 meeting of the Organization of American States. This was the first meeting of the OAS in this country outside of Washington, D.C., and it gave us and our Latin American neighbors an excellent opportunity to know each other better.

We have had a stream of visitors back and forth between our state and Japan, and many successful business contracts have been negotiated during the last few years. Tensions which had been created by textile import competitions have been alleviated completely, and the Japanese have become the major overseas investors in our state. All of us have been impressed with the inclination of Japanese business leaders to honor their verbal commitments, and often to assure that their performance exceeds their promises.

In order to insure the continuing opportunity for penetrating analyses of complicated, important, and timely foreign-policy questions, there is in operation an organization known as the Trilateral Commission. A group of leaders from the three democratic, developed areas of the world meet every six months to discuss ideas of current interest to Japan, North America, and Europe. Subjects like the world monetary system, economic relations between rich and poor nations, world trade, energy, the future of the seas, aid to less-developed countries, and other possibilities for international understanding and cooperation are first studied by scholars, then debated by members of the commission, and finally analyses are published and distributed to world leaders. Membership on this commission has provided me with a splendid learning opportunity, and many of the other members have helped me in my study of foreign affairs.

In our fast-changing technological world, the interrelationships among societal factors are indeed difficult to understand. Increases in world population, food shortages, environmental deterioration, depletion of irreplaceable commodities, trade barriers and market price disruptions, arms buildups, arguments over control of the seas, and many other similar problems are each serious in themselves, but each has a complicating effect on the others. Because we are so powerful, our actions have a great impact on other nations even when such effect is not our intention. There is no possible means of isolating ourselves from the rest of the world, so we must provide leadership. But this leadership need not depend on our inherent military force, or economic power, or political persuasion. It should derive from the fact that we try to be right and honest and truthful and decent.

The effectuation of an enlightened foreign policy can be realized only if we can get our domestic house in order and have all the policies of our government dependent on the educated and freely expressed will of the American people.

There is no need for lying. Our best national defense is the truth.

FOURTEEN

The Person in Front of You

We have a tendency to exalt ourselves and to dwell on the weaknesses and mistakes of others. I have come to realize that in every person there is something fine and pure and noble, along with a desire for self-fulfillment. Political and religious leaders must attempt to provide a society within which these human attributes can be nurtured and enhanced.

In 1965 my oldest son was graduated from high school, and our whole family took a rare extended vacation. Since all of us were able to speak some Spanish, we decided to go to Mexico, and we spent three weeks just traveling slowly around that country, trying to stay in places where English was not spoken and where we could learn most about the Mexican people. It was the best vacation we ever had, and we thoroughly enjoyed being with the farmers, workers, shopkeepers, priests, and others who lived in the small towns and rural areas.

One day as we drove down one of the main highways, we saw a tiny village in a nearby valley, and the name of it in Spanish was the same as our hometown of Plains. It seemed a nondescript and poverty-stricken little place, and we decided to take a photograph of the road sign with the little hamlet in the background. It was in the desert, and consisted of about ten adobe huts, no trees, and a few goats. As we stood on the side of the road and adjusted the camera, a small group of children about eight or ten years old ran toward us. They surrounded us, held out their hands, and in Spanish begged for something. I told Rosalynn to get out her pocketbook and give them some coins, and then finally understood what they were saying. They were not asking for "dinero," which means "money." They were saying two other words: "lapiz" and "papel," meaning "pencil" and "paper." This moved us deeply, and we gave all the children coins and all the reading and writing material we had in the car.

As we drove on in our air-conditioned automobile, I thought about the hunger of those children to learn more about themselves and about the outside world. They also exemplified to me the people of my own country whose yearnings for a better life have not been realized.

Although we sometimes recognize the responsibility to alleviate affliction and to provide opportunities for those who trust us in positions of leadership, we often take pride in our own strength and self-reliance. We are reluctant to demonstrate emotion or even compassion, for fear of being considered weak.

Once I spent several days working among Spanish-speaking families in a ghetto area of a New England city. I was representing my church and speaking their language to the Cuban and Puerto Rican people who had recently come to our country to live. Since my Spanish had been learned in the navy, the vocabulary was somewhat different, and I worked along with a Cuban Christian named Eloy Cruz. Those whom we visited were initially quite antagonistic and had withdrawn from intimate contact with the surrounding community.

Senor Cruz was a muscular, swarthy, manly person, and one of the best men I have ever known. He had a remarkable ability to reach the hearts of people in a very natural and unassuming way and quickly convinced them that we loved them and that God loved them. I observed him closely as we spent that inspiring week together.

The lives of many people were changed by the words and prayers and laughter and friendship of this good man. We visited one particularly poor home where an elderly couple lived, and we were surprised to find a tiny baby there. They eventually told us that the child's mother had gone to the dentist to have a tooth extracted, had begun to bleed excessively, and had died before the flow of blood could be stopped. Her husband was a young accountant, who had gone berserk when he heard the news of his wife's death. He had tried to commit suicide and threatened to kill the baby. The old couple had volunteered to keep the child. As we left we offered them some money, which at first the man and woman refused. They finally agreed to use it to buy the baby something in memory of its mother.

The final day of my visit was marred by a cold and drizzling rain. I was also saddened at the prospect of leaving Eloy Cruz, perhaps never to see him again. On our last visit of the day, we knocked on the door of a relatively nice apartment building. We were turning to leave the locked door when the landlord came up the street and invited us in for a cup of coffee. He had seen us on the sidewalks of the neighborhood that week and wondered what we were doing.

As we walked up the stairs toward his own apartment, he pointed to a closed door and told us that a young man lived there whose wife had recently died from a freak accident at the dentist's office. He said that the young man would not open the door or speak to anyone. Senor Cruz went to the door and knocked, and the man inside told him to go away. Cruz said, "We know your baby," and the door opened. The slender young man asked, "Are you the men who gave my baby some money?" Later, inside the apartment we had one of the most moving religious experiences of my life.

Back on the street, I was saying goodby to Eloy Cruz, and I asked him how a tough and rugged man like him could be so sensitive, kind, and filled with love. He was embarrassed by my question, but finally fumbled out an answer.

"Senor Jaime, nuestro Salvador tiene los manos que son muy suaves, y El no puede hacer mucho con un hombre que es dura." (Our Savior has hands which are very gentle, and he cannot do much with a man who is hard.)

I thought about this often as governor of Georgia. How can we combine the competent and efficient management of taxpayers' money with the sensitive and effective service needed to alleviate affliction and to enhance the development and use of the capabilities of our most needy citizens?

A Chinese philosopher, Kuan Tzu, who lived about 2000 B.C., expressed it well: "If you give a man a fish, he has one meal. If you teach him how to fish, he can feed himself for life."

Or, as Eloy Cruz often said, "You only need to have two loves: one for God, and one for the person who happens to be standing in front of you at any given moment."

To the extent that we can distinguish between potentially productive social-service recipients and those who are permanently and inherently dependent on government services, we can minister more effectively to both groups. This is the first step toward the development of an acceptable welfare and public-health system, and it is certainly within the capability of the American people.

We also should not underestimate the personal ability and obligation of private citizens to minister to those who are in need. There has been an excessive inclination to wash our hands of this responsibility, and to assume that government alone can deal with the problems of the poor and afflicted.

A few years ago I was sitting in church in Plains thinking about the title of the morning sermon. I do not remember anything our pastor had to say that morning, but I have never forgotten the title of the sermon: "If you were arrested for being a Christian, would there be enough evidence to convict you?"

I was then a member of the largest and most prestigious church in town, a Sunday school teacher and a deacon, and I professed to be quite concerned about my religious duties. But when asked that question, I finally decided that if arrested and charged with being a committed follower of God, I could probably talk my way out of it! It was a sobering thought.

Every year we have a one-week revival service, when a visiting preacher comes in to work with our church members in an evangelistic effort. In preparation for this week the leaders of the church go out into the community and invite the non-church members to worship with us during the revival week. As a deacon, I had always participated in this effort and would go with our pastor or with another deacon on one or two evenings. We would take our Bibles, visit a couple of homes each year, and tell them about the scheduled activities. We would read a Scripture, have a prayer, say a few words about our religious beliefs, talk about the weather and the crops, and depart. I was always proud enough of this effort to retain a clear conscience throughout the remainder of the year.

One day I was invited to speak to a nearby church group in Preston, Georgia, which is a small town with a population of about three hundred (about half that of Plains). The subject assigned to me was "Christian Witnessing." I thought immediately that they had undoubtedly heard about the wonderful work I was doing in my own church.

When I went into the front room to write my speech about witnessing, it was with some sense of self-satisfaction. About halfway through composing the speech I decided to make a real impression on the audience. I began to figure how many individual visits I had made for God. Since it had been fourteen years since I had returned home from the navy, and I had visited an average of two families a year, and assuming two parents and three children per family, there were a total of 140 visits! I proudly wrote the figure down on my notes, and still have it.

While I was congratulating myself, suddenly I remembered the 1966 governor's election. It was very late when we decided to make the campaign, so we had to work furiously to overcome the handicap of the late start. I left everything I cared for—my wife, my family, my farm, my bird dogs—and I spent sixteen to eighteen hours a day trying to reach as many Georgia voters as possible. We went in opposite directions, shaking hands and telling everyone what a wonderful man I was and why they should vote for me. At the end of the almost successful campaign we had met more than 300,000 Georgians.

The comparison struck me—300,000 visits for myself in three months, and 140 visits for God in fourteen years!

I began to read the Bible with a new interest and perspective and to understand more clearly the admonitions about pride and self-satisfaction. I read again the parable (Luke 18:10–13) about the Pharisee who came into the Temple and said: "God, I thank thee that I am not like other men, extortioners, unjust, adulterers, or even like this tax collector. I fast twice a week, I give tithes of all that I get." But the tax collector, standing far off, would not even lift up his eyes to heaven, but beat his breast, saying, "God, be merciful to me a sinner!" For the first time I saw that I was the Pharisee.

I began to expand my personal service in the church and to search more diligently for a closer relationship with God among my different business, professional, and political interests. An invitation came for me to go to another state to witness for a week within about a hundred families among whom there were no believers in God. I was told that no special qualifications were required, just the willingness to give a week of my life to God, "with no strings attached." After accepting the invitation I realized that during the more than thirty years of my church membership there had probably not been one hour of total commitment to God with absolutely "no strings attached." It was an exhilarating week, and similar experiences were repeated in subsequent years.

But there is always the continuing temptation to be content with meager accomplishments in our religious lives, as we lower our standards of service to match worldly expectations or our own convenience. There is also the temptation to judge other people without charity, and I have been tempted to do this since I was a small child.

It is easy, too, to excuse a lack of purposeful service to others by emphasizing our own inadequacies. "I am not qualified to accomplish anything important" is a common attitude for us to assume. This is a mistake.

A few months ago I attended a ceremony in Macon, Georgia, to participate in an award ceremony sponsored by *Guideposts* magazine for the outstanding church in the United States. More than five thousand people had assembled in the civic center to honor the church and to hear Dr. Norman Vincent Peale speak. He made a powerful and moving speech, and I also did the best I could to make a good impression on the large audience. The church which was honored had thirty-five members, all of them mentally retarded. It is called the Church of the Exceptional.

To conclude the ceremony, a forty-five-year-old mongoloid woman came slowly down the aisle with a torch in her hand. As was her assignment each week, she struggled that evening to light the one large candle at the foot of the stage. Her eyesight was poor, and her hand was not steady. She could not light the candle. We all leaned forward in sympathy and concern. The pastor moved forward to assist her, and her face showed that she was stricken with disappointment.

Then the candle lit!

The whole assembly breathed a sigh of relief, and as she turned around with a beautiful expression on her happy face, she touched the hearts of everyone there. This demonstration of her simple and total commitment to her duty had more power and persuasion than any of the well-prepared and erudite words any of us had to offer.

We must constantly search for ways to make our own lives more significant and more meaningful, regardless of our apparent lack of talent or influence. A great modern-day theologian, Paul Tillich, said in one of his profound books that religion is the search for the truth about man's existence and his relationship to God. He pointed out that when we think we know it all and are satisfied with what we have accomplished in the eyes of God, we are already far from God.

It is not easy to make this self-assessment. Recently I was in a large city to speak at their annual chamber of commerce banquet. The leaders of the community were trying to induce some Indians to move to the city from a reservation in the West to manage a local Indian mound area which had been restored as a tourist attraction. They were concerned about how the Indians might be accepted in the community and whether they would be happy there. After determining their religious belief, I said, "Why not go down to your largest downtown church and see if the welcoming committee will go out to visit the reservation and invite the Indians to attend church services when they come here? This would be an excellent way to assure them that they will be welcome and accepted."

They thought about it awhile, and then said, "Well, maybe we ought to try it first with one of our suburban churches, because our downtown church is not integrated. We don't know how they will feel about Indians." Their community self-assessment was made. Our personal problems are magnified when we assume different standards of morality and ethics in our own lives as we shift from one responsibility or milieu to another. Should elected officials assume different levels of concern, compassion, or love toward their own family or loved ones? Should a businessman like me have a lower standard of honesty and integrity in dealing with my customers than I assume as a Sunday school teacher or a church deacon? Of course not. But we do.

Our own personal standards are varied, but the expectations we have for politics and government are even more disturbing. We are quite often happy to achieve mediocrity in government. This low expectation, admittedly based on unhappy experience, can only contribute to the perpetuation of low standards of achievement. There is no legitimate reason why government should not represent the highest possible common ideals and characteristics of the people who form and support it. Its example should be inspirational and not embarrassing. Its hopes and aspirations should mirror those of its finest subjects. Equity and fairness should be basic and unquestioned. Are these characteristics impossible to achieve? No. They should be the least that we demand.

Of course, it is important to have an effective mechanism of government. There is no way to insure justice, reduce crime, tax equitably, relieve suffering, protect the quality of life, transport cargo and people, marshal a common effort, or maintain peace without a trusted and competent government. If we insist that the Golden Rule be applied in all public matters, then potential inequities can be prevented, and wrongs can be righted. A simple and well-structured government, operating with minimum secrecy and with its goals and policies clearly expressed, will be much more likely to represent what we as people are or ought to be. To establish and maintain such a government is the proper purpose of public service.

FIFTEEN

Presidential Plans

I have always looked on the presidency of the United States with reverence and awe, and I still do. But recently I have begun to realize that the president is just a human being. I can almost remember when I began to change my mind and form this opinion.

Before becoming governor I had never met a president, although I once saw Harry Truman at a distance. He was present when we laid the keel of the first atomic submarine, *Nautilus*, in New London, Connecticut, in 1952. Great presidents like Washington, Jefferson, Lincoln, and Roosevelt have always been historical figures to me, and even the intimate biographical information published about them has never made them seem quite human.

Then during 1971 and 1972 I met Richard Nixon, Spiro Agnew, George McGovern, Henry Jackson, Hubert Humphrey, Ed Muskie, George Wallace, Ronald Reagan, Nelson Rockefeller, and other presidential hopefuls, and I lost my feeling of awe about presidents. This is not meant as a criticism of them, but it is merely a simple statement of fact.

After the 1972 convention I began with the help of those close to me to think seriously about a presidential campaign, and to assess my own strengths and weaknesses. In fact, the frank assessment of my shortcomings became one of the most enjoyable experiences for my staff, my friends, and my family, and was a time-consuming process. We talked about politics, geography, character, education, experience, appearance, age, mannerisms,

Jimmy and Rosalynn launch the campaign for president.

and lack of fame. In spite of these critical assessments, I decided to run.

Let me try to relate a brief list of the kinds of things we discussed.

1. I am a farmer. That seemed a disadvantage to some, but the other side was that this would not hurt the farm vote, a real factor. Moreover, over the period of a lifetime, being a farmer makes one willing to face apparently insuperable difficulties and still take a chance even though the future—the weather, the economy, the variables—may seem just one big gamble. Also, I can claim with credentials to be an engineer, a planner, a nuclear physicist, a businessman, and a professional naval officer. So, for those who might have an aversion to farmers, for whatever reason, there are some alternative ways of looking at what my candidacy has to offer.

2. I live in the Deep South, and no Southerner has been elected president in more than a hundred years. And yet I remember fifteen years ago when the political analysts said that Southerners would never vote for an Irish Catholic from Boston, but when the

returns were counted in 1960, John Kennedy got a bigger margin of victory—not in Massachusetts but in Georgia! Also, in a predominantly white voter district in 1972, we elected a man who came into his first public visibility as the young field worker for Martin Luther King, Jr.—Congressman Andrew Young. In 1974, even as a freshman congressman, his opposition for a second term was hardly detectable. Sectional or geographical prejudice is becoming a minimal political factor.

More disadvantages:

1. My home is Plains, Georgia, population about 600. This gives me little urban base; but in microcosm, nonetheless, our people in Plains represent very well the people of the nation—and I know all of the Plains people. We live and work together in a spirit of friendship and harmony.

Our 250 white citizens and our 350 black citizens learn from one another and always have. There may even be some political advantage with voters because rural people sometimes have the

Plains Depot, the campaign headquarters

reputation (perhaps undeserved) of living close to the earth, close to God, close to poverty, and closer to their government. Anyhow, Plains has about the same population density as Atlanta: about 800 people to the square mile.

2. I would not be holding office while running for the White House in 1976; but this would give me full time to campaign, unlike members of Congress who at least in theory would be obliged to pay attention to their proper responsibilities in Washington.

3. The national news media are concentrated in Washington, a disadvantage for a former Georgia governor, age fifty, politically unemployed. True again, as a disadvantage, but on the other hand there are 535 members of Congress reaching for every microphone and struggling for every headline.

In the meantime, I reasoned, I likely would be the only presidential candidate that day in Sioux City, or in St. Petersburg, Phoenix, or Rochester. Furthermore, a lot of national newspeople stop over in Georgia and Atlanta on their way to Montgomery for their monthly interview with Alabama governor George Wallace! Maybe, later, the word might drift back to Washington about me.

4. A fault: I don't know how to compromise on any principle I believe is right. Georgia secretary of state Ben Fortson, probably the most respected, statewide-elected official in my home state, a white-haired patriarch who speaks as eloquently about American history as any man I have ever heard, once called me "as stubborn as a South Georgia turtle." Unthinking noncompromise is foolish; but maybe this is a time, on matters of principle, for an absence of compromise.

5. Others might have a head start on financing. True enough; three other candidates had already raised more than a million dollars before the new campaign-finance law went into effect. Yet with a small, effective staff and the hope of a large group of politically attractive volunteers, plus plenty of personal effort by me and my family, and a total commitment to campaign full time

throughout the nation, it seemed likely that it would be possible to attract enough financial support to help win the nomination and the election.

How does one prepare for such an undertaking? The first step was to assess my own current and ongoing responsibilities which had to be fulfilled. As governor of Georgia I had completed the most critical and demanding portion of my term, but there were hundreds of administrative duties which I enjoyed and which I had to perform. My routine of arriving at the capitol office early and working a full day continued until I completed my final day in office. But I began to discern from the governor's job special experiences which would be similar to those of a president. The administration of federal programs involving welfare, health, education, transportation, environment, recreation, energy, housing, and urban renewal took on additional meanings. Long-range planning techniques, budgeting procedures, government organization, tax measures, prison reform, criminal justice, foreign trade, and social problems became more challenging subjects as they were analyzed for comparative application to both state and federal government service delivery systems.

I had always read three or four books each week, and it was easy and natural to revise my reading lists to encompass subjects relating more toward foreign affairs, defense, and economics. I accumulated and read histories and biographies concerning our nation and the presidency, and, in order to avoid mistakes, even studied the campaign platforms of all the unsuccessful candidates for president since our electoral process began.

I read scientific journals about every conceivable source of energy, so I might understand the potential for meeting the world's needs during the decades ahead. Nuclear disarmament proposals and agreements were studied, along with budgets of the different services within the defense department. A special effort was made to meet the authors of these books and articles, so I might obtain more information about their subjects first hand. Later several of them provided me with prepublication drafts of their writings. Service on the Trilateral Commission gave me an

excellent opportunity to know national and international leaders in many fields of study concerning foreign affairs.

We continued to accumulate names of those who attended the
numerous conventions in Atlanta. Since part of my job as governor was to give a welcoming talk or a more substantive speech, it
was easy for us to ask for a list of the conventioneers and their home
addresses. Foreign travel and my numerous meetings with visitors
from other nations became more interesting to me, and I used each
such opportunity as a means for studying the country involved.

As chairman of the National Democratic Party 1974 Campaign
Committee it was my responsibility to learn as much as possible
about all the states and congressional districts involved in the
elections. We began to monitor the thirty-five gubernatorial campaigns, the thirty-four campaigns for U.S. senator, and all of the
435 elections for Congress. During 1973 and 1974, I met frequently
with leaders of groups who ordinarily support Democratic candidates. These leaders, from about twenty-five different organizations, represented labor unions, farmers, Spanish Americans,
teachers, environmentalists, women, local officials, retired persons, government workers, blacks, and the House and Senate campaign committees.

Four or five of the major opinion pollsters worked closely with
me and helped to delineate the most important issues among the
American electorate as the elections approached. With the help
of a volunteer staff, we recruited several experts in each of about
thirty issue subjects to give me their opinions of what our nation
should do about that particular question, and then we edited those
disparate suggestions into one coherent issue paper on each subject. These were printed in a standard format and mailed out to
more than one thousand Democratic candidates for high political
office. Later, after the primaries were over and nominees of our
party had been selected, I went out into more than sixty campaigns to work personally with the candidates and their staffs. Our
staff members from the Democratic National Committee worked
in dozens of other campaigns. All of this was also a good learning
experience for me.

A major factor in any political campaign is always the identity and characteristics of potential opponents, and we discussed in some detail those who might run for president in 1976. There was never any hesitancy about our plans because of other prospective candidates.

Our strategy was simple: make a total effort all over the nation. After leaving office as governor, during the first months alone, I visited more than half the states, some of them several times. Each visit was carefully planned—by my small Atlanta staff and a local volunteer in each community—to be included during the week's trip. Our purposes during this early stage of the campaign were to become known among those who have a continuing interest in politics and government, to recruit supporters and raise campaign funds, and to obtain maximum news coverage for myself and for my stand on the many local and national issues. The most important purpose of all was for me to learn this nation—what it is, and what it ought to be.

Our trips proved to be interesting and educational—and politically successful. One of the standard events which we scheduled was a meeting with the full editorial boards of the major newspapers and magazines of our country. There seemed to be a standard format. We would sit down to lunch promptly at a scheduled time, in a private dining room within the office building of the publication. As the first course of salad or soup was served, the questions began. They continued in an uninterrupted stream until the session adjourned about two hours later. I could never find time to eat a bite, although dishes of delicious-looking food were placed in front of me and the others, and then later removed after the editors had eaten theirs. Among the more competent groups, specialists among the editors and news reporters had carefully prepared their questions on issues of national and international interest. These meetings were invariably enjoyable to me and greatly helped me to understand which issues were of most importance in that particular section of the nation or among the readers of that magazine or newspaper.

My staff learned to have a hamburger and a milkshake waiting after the luncheon, so I could eat on the way to our next appointment.

Jimmy Carter

I have thought about New Hampshire a lot, maybe for the obvious reason that it does have that tradition of the first state presidential primary in the nation, and I like the state. Our family lived in New England at three different times while we were in the navy, so we naturally felt at home in that region. But there does seem to be something special about the people of New Hampshire and their attitude toward politics and the presidential primary. It is a major industry for them every four years, as candidates, staffs, volunteers, and news reporters traipse from one community to the other during our first primary contest. A few of the political "workers" in the state just want to be entertained by presidential aspirants, want to meet all of them to complete a check-off list, or want to see their own names in the *New York Times*. But these political dilettantes are rare.

It was amazing to me as I began campaigning how few of the people in New Hampshire have actually seen a candidate for president. Apparently most of the campaigning in the past has been superficial and arranged mostly for the benefit of the news media. It has always been my custom to go directly to the people where they live or work. On my first two visits, I campaigned at prominent downtown bus stops and then went through the stores and government office buildings in Manchester and in Concord when the people arrived at work. Local workers in the state's largest city and many state workers in the capitol said to me they had never before been visited by a national candidate! A few of them had seen Pat Paulsen in 1972. In factories, in churches, in schools, and in shopping centers I found the people much more aware of the then-distant election than in other states, and much more interested in meeting me and in knowing about my campaign.

As my visits to the different states continued, I became more and more convinced of the inherent and unshakable greatness of our country. For instance, my ancestors and I have always been farmers, and this is one subject which I have studied and practiced as a profession. But I have been thrilled again and again as I met those Americans who produce artichokes in California, syrup in Vermont, cheese in Wisconsin, wheat in Kansas, beef in Nebraska, sweet corn in Florida, rice in Louisiana, sugar in Minnesota, tobacco in Connecticut, and honey in Iowa.

SIXTEEN

Those Two Questions Again

Dozens of issues are considered during a political campaign, but candidates do not create the issues. They exist in the minds and hearts of our citizens. It is exceedingly interesting and sometimes surprising to learn which subjects are of most interest and which questions are of the most concern. In the first chapter of this book, I stated the two basic and generic questions:

Can our government be honest, decent, open, fair, and compassionate?

Can our government be competent?

The first question springs from a quiet bewilderment and personal sense that we have lost something precious which formerly made us proud. In my judgment, the answer to that question is a resounding YES, provided we can succeed in stripping away secrecy and letting our government be what our people are. Politically, this question does not have a sharp cutting edge, because any candidate who personally professes to be honest immediately reminds the listeners of the pious pronouncements and protestations of our convicted former leaders.

For too long political leaders have been isolated from the people. They have made decisions from an ivory tower. Few have ever seen personally the direct impact of government programs involving welfare, prisons, mental institutions, unemployment, school busing, or public housing. Our people feel that they have little access to the core of government and little influence with elected officials.

Now it is time for this chasm between people and government to be bridged and for American citizens to join in shaping our nation's future.

Now is the time for new commitments and new ideas to make a reality of these dreams, still held by our people.

To begin with, the confidence of people in our own government must be restored. But too many officials do not deserve that confidence.

There is a simple and effective way for public officials to regain public trust—be trustworthy!

But there are also specific steps that must be taken.

Politicians who seek to further their political careers through appeals to our doubts, fears, and prejudices must be exposed and rejected.

We need all-inclusive sunshine laws so that special interests will not retain their exclusive access behind closed government doors. Except in a few rare cases, there is no reason for secret meetings of regulatory agencies, other executive departments, or congressional committees. Such meetings must be opened to the public, all votes recorded, and complete news media coverage authorized and encouraged.

Absolutely no gifts of value should ever again be permitted to a public official.

Complete revelation of all business and financial involvements of major officials should be required, and none should be continued which constitute a possible conflict with the public interest.

Regulatory agencies must not be managed by representatives of the industry being regulated, and no personnel transfers between agency and the industry should be made within a period of four full years.

Public financing of campaigns should be extended to members of Congress.

The activities of lobbyists must be more thoroughly revealed and controlled.

Minimum secrecy within government should be matched with maximum personal privacy for citizens.

All federal judges, diplomats, and other major officials should be selected on a strict basis of merit.

For many years in the State Department we have chosen from among almost 16,000 applicants about 110 of our nation's finest young leaders to represent us in the international world. But we top this off with the disgraceful and counterproductive policy of appointing unqualified persons to major diplomatic posts as political payoffs. This must be stopped immediately.

Every effort should be extended to encourage full participation by our people in their own government's processes, including universal voter registration for elections.

We must insure better public understanding of executive policy and better exchange of ideas between the Congress and the White House. To do this, cabinet members representing the president should meet in scheduled and televised public interrogation sessions with the full bodies of Congress.

All our citizens must know that they will be treated fairly.

As important as honesty and openness are—they are not enough. There must also be substance and logical direction in government.

The second basic question, "Can our government be competent?" is more definitive and concrete. Evidence seems to be plentiful that the answer is NO, but the answer again is YES. Many of our leading politicians, news reporters, political scientists, and business executives doubt that government can be efficient, fair, and economical. But it can. Drastic changes will be necessary, but such governmental action is not unprecedented. Many state and local governments have devised clear and simple organizational structures, effective and incisive budgeting techniques, comprehensive planning procedures, and ready access to the core of government by its own private citizens. I have personal experience which convinces me that these improvements can be effectuated in Washington.

The mechanism of our government should be understandable, efficient, and economical . . . and it can be.

We must give top priority to a drastic and thorough revision of the federal bureaucracy, to its budgeting system, and to the procedures for constantly analyzing the effectiveness of its many varied services. Tight, businesslike management and planning techniques must be instituted and maintained, utilizing the full authority and personal involvement of the president himself.

This is no job for the fainthearted. It will be met with violent opposition from those who now enjoy a special privilege, those who prefer to work in the dark, or those whose private fiefdoms are threatened.

We must abolish and consolidate hundreds of obsolete and unnecessary federal programs and agencies. We must evolve clearly defined goals and policies in every part of government. We must implement an effective system of zero-based budgeting and institute tough performance auditing to insure proper conduct and efficient delivery of services.

Steps like these can insure a full return on our hard-earned tax dollars. These procedures are working in state capitols around the nation and in our successful businesses, both large and small.

They can and they will work in Washington.

They cannot be made timidly or incrementally. Proposals must be fair and equitable, and simple enough to be understood. The natural opposition of special interests, selfish bureaucrats, and hidebound elected officials must be overcome. This is not as difficult as it might seem. These opponents simply cannot prevail against the truth and an aroused and determined public. I have often seen them retreat into their dark corners when exposed to public scrutiny and debate.

I have also seen staunch allies emerge from among those who would ordinarily be expected to oppose such change. Most professional government workers are competent and dedicated and realize acutely that a confused and complicated bureaucracy prevents them from the effective performance of their life's chosen work. Most of them have been very supportive of organizational and programmatic improvements when presented with a clear vision of what might be accomplished.

When we reorganized the Georgia government, administrative

costs were reduced by more than half, and in some departments substantial reductions in personnel billets were made. There was a strong shift from administration toward personal delivery of service to citizens. During this entire process, no merit-system employee was discharged because of government reorganization. Many of the vacancies caused by routine resignations, transfers, and retirements were simply not refilled. Many workers were transferred to more productive jobs, but complaints were few.

Even the special-interest groups who had enjoyed privileges under former administrations proved that they preferred to leave behind the obligation to seek special favors in the dark of political intrigue.

Attempts to reform systems of cash management, taxation, health, welfare, education, transportation, or governmental management are doomed unless they are bold and comprehensive. With small and incremental changes, there is an intensive focusing of effort to oppose the change by those who are benefiting from the status quo. There is rarely any public interest in the subject when it is technical or narrowly defined. The special interests almost invariably prevail. But if political leaders can understand what is right and fair, devise a comprehensive plan for improvement, and describe to the public clearly what should be done, then even the most far-reaching reforms are possible.

To alleviate the understandable concerns about the competence of our government is a tremendous challenge. This is a political issue of utmost importance.

Our nation now has no understandable national purpose, no clearly defined goals, and no organizational mechanism to develop or achieve such purposes or goals. We move from one crisis to the next as if they were fads, even though the previous one hasn't been solved.

The Bible says: "If the trumpet give an uncertain sound, who shall prepare himself to the battle?" As a planner and a businessman, and a chief executive, I know from experience that uncertainty is also a devastating affliction in private life and in government. Coordination of different programs is impossible. There is no clear vision of what is to be accomplished, everyone struggles for temporary advantage, and there is no way to monitor how effectively services are delivered.

What is our national policy for the production, acquisition, distribution, or consumption of energy in times of shortage or doubtful supply?

There is no policy!

What are our long-range goals in health care, transportation, land use, economic development, waste disposal, or housing?

There are no goals!

The tremendous resources of our people and of our chosen leaders can be harnessed to devise effective, understandable, and practical goals and policies in every realm of public life.

A government that is honest and competent, with clear purpose and strong leadership, can work with the American people to meet the challenges of the present and the future.

We can then face together the tough long-range solutions to our economic woes. Our people are ready to make personal sacrifices when clear national economic policies are devised and understood.

We are grossly wasting our energy resources and other precious raw materials as though their supply were infinite. We must even face the prospect of changing our basic ways of living. This change will either be made on our own initiative in a planned and rational way or forced on us with chaos and suffering by the inexorable laws of nature.

Energy imports and consumption must be reduced, free competition enhanced by rigid enforcement of antitrust laws, and general monetary growth restrained. Pinpointed federal programs can ease the more acute pains of recession. The federal budget must be controlled, and long-range financing should be provided for any service programs so that the budget can be balanced.

We are still floundering and equivocating about protection of our environment. Neither designers of automobiles, mayors of cities, power companies, farmers, nor those of us who simply breathe the air, love beauty, and would like to fish or swim in pure water have the slightest idea what is coming out of Washington next! What does come next must be a firm commitment to pure air, clean water, and unspoiled land.

Almost twenty years after its conception we have not finished the basic interstate highway system. To many lobbyists who haunt the capitol buildings of the nation, ground transportation still means only more highways and more automobiles—the bigger, the better. We must have a national commitment to transportation capabilities which will encourage the most efficient movement of American people and cargo.

Gross tax inequities are being perpetuated. The most surely taxed income is that which is derived from the sweat of manual labor. Carefully contrived loopholes let the total tax burden shift more and more toward the average wage earner. The largest corporations pay the lowest tax rates, and some with very high profits pay no tax at all.

When a business executive can charge off a $50 luncheon on a tax return and a truck driver cannot deduct his $1.50 sandwich, when oil companies pay less than 5 percent on their earnings while employees of the company pay at least three times this rate, when many pay no taxes on incomes of more than $100,000, then we need basic tax reform!

Every American has a right to expect that laws will be administered in an evenhanded manner, but it seems that something is wrong even with our system of justice. Defendants who are repeatedly out on bail commit more crimes. Aggravating trial delays and endless litigation are common.

Citizens without influence often bear the brunt of prosecution, while violators of antitrust laws and other white-collar criminals are ignored and go unpunished.

Following recent presidential elections, our U.S. attorney general has replaced the postmaster general as the chief political appointee; and we have recently witnessed the prostitution of this most important law-enforcement office. Special prosecutors had to be appointed simply to insure enforcement of the law! The attorney general should be removed from politics.

The vast bureaucracy of government often fails to deliver needed social services to our people. High ideals and good intentions are not matched with rational, businesslike administration. The predictable result is frustration and discouragement among dedicated employees, recipients of services, and the American taxpayers.

There are about 25 million Americans who are classified as poor, two-thirds of whom happen to be white, and half of whom receive welfare benefits. At least 10 percent of these are able to work. A massive bureaucracy of 2 million employees at all levels of government is attempting to administer more than one hundred different programs of bewildering complexity. Case workers shuffle papers in a morass of red tape. Often it is financially profitable not to work and even to have a family disrupted by forcing the father to leave home. Some combined welfare payments exceed the average working family's income, while other needy families have difficulty obtaining a bare subsistence.

The word "welfare" no longer signifies how much we care but often arouses feelings of contempt and even hatred.

Is a simplified, fair, and compassionate welfare program beyond the capacity of our American government? I think not.

The quality of health care in this nation depends largely on economic status. It is often unavailable or costs too much. There is little commonality of effort between private and public health agencies, or between physicians and other trained medical personnel. Each Congress intends to pass a national health-insurance law. But present government interest seems to be in merely shifting the costs of existing services to the federal taxpayer, or to the employers. There is little interest in preventing the cripplers and killers of our people and providing improved health care for those who still need it most.

Is a practical and comprehensive national health program beyond the capacity of our American government? I think not.

Federal education laws must be simplified to substitute education for paper-shuffling grantsmanship. Local systems need federal funds to supplement their programs for students where wealth and tax base are inequitable.

Is a comprehensive education program beyond the capacity of the American people? I think not.

As a farmer, I have been appalled at the maladministration of our nation's agricultural economy. We have seen the elimination of our valuable food reserves, which has contributed to wild fluctuations in commodity prices and has wiped out dependable trade and export capabilities. Grain speculators and monopolistic processors have profited, while farmers are going bankrupt trying to produce food that consumers are going broke trying to buy.

I know this nation can develop an agricultural policy which will insure a fair profit to our farmers and a fair price to consumers.

It is obvious that domestic and foreign affairs are directly interrelated. A necessary base for effective implementation of any foreign policy is to get our domestic house in order.

Coordination of effort among the leaders of our nation should be established so that our farm production, industrial development, foreign trade, defense, energy, and diplomatic policies are mutually supportive and not in conflict.

The time for American intervention in all the problems of the world is over. But we cannot retreat into isolationism. Ties of friendship and cooperation with our friends and neighbors must be strengthened. Our common interests must be understood and pursued. Highly personalized and narrowly focused diplomatic efforts, although sometimes successful, should be balanced with a more wide-ranging implementation of foreign policy by competent foreign-service officers.

Our nation's security is obviously of paramount importance, and everything must be done to insure adequate military preparedness. But there is no reason why our national defense establishment cannot also be efficient.

Waste and inefficiency are both costly to taxpayers and a danger to our own national existence. Strict management and budgetary control over the Pentagon should reduce the ratio of officers to men and of support forces to combat troops. I see no reason why the Chief of Naval Operations needs more navy captains and commanders on his staff than we have serving on all ships at sea!

Misdirected efforts such as the construction of unnecessary pork-barrel projects by the Corps of Engineers must be terminated.

The biggest waste and danger of all is the unnecessary proliferation of atomic weapons throughout the world. Our ultimate goal should be the elimination of nuclear-weapon capability

The Carter family in 1976

among all nations. In the meantime, simple, careful, and firm proposals to implement this mutual arms reduction should be pursued as a prime national purpose in all our negotiations with nuclear powers—present or potential.

Is the achievement of these and other goals beyond the capacity of our American government? I think not.

Our people are hungry for integrity and competence in government. In this confused and fast-changing technological world we still have within us the capability for national greatness.

Recently we have discovered that our trust has been betrayed. The veils of secrecy have seemed to thicken around Washington. The purposes and goals of our country are uncertain and sometimes even suspect.

Our people are understandably concerned about this lack of competence and integrity. The root of the problem is not so much that our people have lost confidence in government, but that government has demonstrated time and again its lack of confidence in the people.

Our political leaders have simply underestimated the innate quality and character of our people.

It is time for us to reaffirm and to strengthen our ethical and spiritual and political beliefs.

There must be no lowering of these standards, no acceptance of mediocrity in any aspect of our private or public lives.

It is obvious that the best way for our leaders to restore their credibility is to be credible, and in order for us to be trusted we must be trustworthy!

In our homes or at worship we are ever reminded of what we ought to do and what we ought to be. Our government can and must represent the best and the highest ideals of those of us who voluntarily submit to its authority.

In our nation's third century, we must meet these simple but crucial standards.

Why not the best?

Epilogue

I wrote this book at the beginning of what I knew would be a long and sometimes difficult campaign for the presidency. That campaign is over now, and I have been successful. It has not been an easy two years, but I never became discouraged because I never lost faith in either the political process or the people of this country.

The people of America have received me and my family well, with friendship and support. Tens of thousands of volunteers joined and worked with us during the primaries and the general election. I have traveled almost one-half million miles, entered thirty primaries, and made about two thousand speeches. But it has never been an ordeal; nor have we ever considered it to be a sacrifice. All of us learned a lot about our country, and love and respect it more than ever.

Several books have been written about me, and others are now being published about our campaign. I do not intend to write such a book, although excerpts from my speeches will be published soon.

Historic political events have occurred, but the basic themes which I expressed in early chapters of this book have changed very little. My acceptance speech at the Democratic Convention is a good summary of my feelings about our country and its future. It is an appropriate epilogue to *Why Not the Best?*

Jimmy Carter
November 20, 1976

My name is Jimmy Carter, and I'm running for president.

It's been a long time since I said those words the first time, and now I've come here, after seeing our great country, to accept your nomination.

I accept it, in the words of John F. Kennedy, "with a full and grateful heart and with only one obligation: to devote every effort of body, mind and spirit to lead our party back to victory and our nation back to greatness."

It's a pleasure to be here with all you Democrats and to see that our bicentennial celebration and our bicentennial convention has been one of decorum and order without any fights or free-for-alls. Among Democrats, that can only happen once every two hundred years. With this kind of a united Democratic Party, we are ready and eager to take on the Republicans—whichever Republican Party they decide to send against us in November.

Nineteen seventy-six will not be a year of politics as usual. It can be a year of inspiration and hope, and it will be a year of concern, of quiet and sober reassessment of our nation's character and purpose—a year when voters have already confounded the experts. And I guarantee you that it will be the year when we give the government of this country back to the people of this country.

There is a new mood in America. We have been shaken by a tragic war abroad and by scandals and broken promises at home. Our people are searching for new voices and new ideas and new leaders.

Although government has its limits and cannot solve all our problems, we Americans reject the view that we must be reconciled to failures and mediocrity, or to an inferior quality of life. For I believe that we can come through this time of trouble stronger than ever. Like troops who have been in combat, we have been tempered in the fire; we have been disciplined, and we have been educated. Guided by lasting and simple moral values, we have emerged idealists without illusions, realists who still know the old dreams of justice and liberty, of country and of community.

This year we have had thirty state primaries—more than ever before—making it possible to take our campaign directly to the people of America: to homes and shopping centers, to factory shift lines and colleges, to beauty parlors and barber shops, to farmers' markets and union halls.

This has been a long and a personal campaign—a humbling experience, reminding us that ultimate political influence rests not with the power brokers but with the people. This has been a time for learning and for the exchange of ideas, a time of tough debate on the important issues facing our country. This kind of debate is part of our tradition, and as Democrats we are heirs to a great tradition.

I have never met a Democratic president, but I have always been a Democrat.

Years ago, as a farm boy sitting outdoors with my family on the ground in the middle of the night, gathered close around a battery radio connected to the automobile battery and listening to the Democratic conventions in far-off cities, I was a long way from the selection process then. I feel much closer to it tonight.

Ours is the party of the man who was nominated by those distant conventions and who inspired and restored this nation in its darkest hours—Franklin D. Roosevelt.

Ours is the party of a fighting Democrat who showed us that a common man could be an uncommon leader—Harry S Truman.

Ours is the party of a brave young president who called the young at heart, regardless of age, to seek a "New Frontier" of national greatness —John F. Kennedy.

And ours is also the party of a greathearted Texan who took office in a tragic hour and who went on to do more than any other president in this century to advance the cause of human rights—Lyndon Johnson.

Our party was built out of the sweatshops of the old Lower East Side [of Manhattan], the dark mills of New Hampshire, the blazing hearths of Illinois, the coal mines of Pennsylvania, the hardscrabble farms of the southern coastal plains, and the unlimited frontiers of America.

Ours is the party that welcomed generations of immigrants—the Jews, the Irish, the Italians, the Poles, and all the others—enlisted them in its ranks, and fought the political battles that helped bring them into the American mainstream. And they have shaped the character of our party.

That is our heritage. Our party has not been perfect. We have made mistakes, and we have paid for them. But ours is a tradition of leadership and compassion and progress.

Our leaders have fought for every piece of progressive legislation, from RFD [rural free delivery of mail] and REA [Rural Electrification Administration] to Social Security and civil rights. In times of need, the Democrats were there.

But in recent years, our nation has seen a failure of leadership. We have been hurt, and we have been disillusioned. We have seen a wall go up that separates us from our own government.

We have lost some precious things that historically have bound our people and our government together. We feel that moral decay has weakened our country, that it is crippled by a lack of goals and values, and that our public officials have lost faith in us.

We have been a nation adrift too long. We have been without leadership too long. We have had divided and deadlocked government too long. We have been governed by veto too long. We have suffered enough at the hands of a tired and worn-out administration without new ideas, without youth or vitality, without vision, and without the confidence of the American people.

There is a fear that our best years are behind us. But I say to you that our nation's best is still ahead.

Our country has lived through a time of torment. It is now a time for healing. We want to have faith again! We want to be proud again! We just want the *truth* again!

It is time for the people to run the government, and not the other way around.

It is time to honor and strengthen our families and our neighborhoods and our diverse cultures and customs.

We need a Democratic president and a Congress to work in harmony for a change, with mutual respect for a change, in the open for a change. And next year we are going to have that new leadership. You can depend on it!

It is time for America to move and to speak, not with boasting and belligerence but with a quiet strength, to depend in world affairs not merely on the size of an arsenal but on the nobility of ideas, and to govern at home not by confusion and crisis but with grace and imagination and common sense.

Too many have had to suffer at the hands of the political and economic elite who have shaped decisions and never had to account for mistakes nor to suffer from injustice. When unemployment prevails, they never stand in line looking for a job. When deprivation results from a confused and bewildering welfare system, they never do without food or clothing or a place to sleep. When the public schools are inferior or torn by strife, their children go to exclusive private schools. And when the bureaucracy is bloated and confused, the powerful always manage to discover and occupy niches of special influence and privilege. An unfair tax structure serves their needs. And tight secrecy always seems to prevent reform.

All of us must be careful not to cheat each other. Too often, unholy, self-perpetuating alliances have been formed between money and politics, and the average citizen has been held at arm's length.

Each time our nation has made a serious mistake, the American people have been excluded from the process. The tragedy of Vietnam and Cambodia, the disgrace of Watergate, and the embarrassment of the CIA revelations could have been avoided if our government had simply reflected the sound judgment and good common sense and the high moral character of the American people.

It is time for us to take a new look at our own government, to strip away the secrecy, to expose the unwarranted pressure of lobbyists, to eliminate waste, to release our civil servants from bureaucratic chaos, to provide tough management, and always to remember that in any town or city the mayor, the governor, and the president represent exactly the same constituents.

As a governor, I had to deal each day with the complicated and confused and overlapping and wasteful federal government bureaucracy. As president, I want you to help me evolve an efficient, economical, purposeful, and manageable government for our nation. Now, I recognize the difficulty, but if I'm elected, it's going to be done. And you can depend on it!

We must strengthen the government closest to the people. Business, labor, agriculture, education, science, and government should not struggle in isolation from one another, but should be able to strive toward mutual goals and shared opportunities. We should make major investments in people and not in buildings and weapons. The poor, the aged, the weak, the afflicted must be treated with respect and compassion and with love.

I have spoken a lot of times this year about love. But love must be aggressively translated into simple justice. The test of any government is not how popular it is with the powerful, but how honestly and fairly it deals with those who must depend on it.

It is time for a complete overhaul of our income-tax system. I still tell you: It is a disgrace to the human race. All my life I have heard promises about tax reform, but it never quite happens. With your help, we are finally going to make it happen. And you can depend on it!

Here is something that can really help our country: It is time for universal voter registration.

It is time for a nationwide, comprehensive health program for all our people.

It is time to guarantee an end to discrimination because of race or sex by full involvement in the decision-making processes of government by those who know what it is to suffer from discrimination. And they'll be in the government if I am elected.

It is time for the law to be enforced. We cannot educate children, we cannot create harmony among our people, we cannot preserve basic human freedom unless we have an orderly society.

Now, crime and lack of justice are especially cruel to those who are least able to protect themselves. Swift arrest and trial, fair and uniform punishment should be expected by anyone who would break our laws.

It is time for our government leaders to respect the law no less than the humblest citizen, so that we can end once and for all a double standard of justice. I see no reason why big-shot crooks should go free and the poor ones go to jail.

A simple and a proper function of government is just to make it easy for us to do good and difficult for us to do wrong.

Now, as an engineer, a planner, a businessman, I see clearly the value to our nation of a strong system of free enterprise based on increased productivity and adequate wages. We Democrats believe that competition is better than regulation, and we intend to combine strong safeguards for consumers with minimal intrusion of government in our free economic system.

I believe that anyone who is able to work ought to work—and ought to have a chance to work. We will never have an end to the inflationary spiral, we will never have a balanced budget—which I am determined to see—as long as we have eight or nine million Americans out of work who cannot find a job. Now, any system of economics is bankrupt if it sees either value or virtue in unemployment. We simply cannot check inflation by keeping people out of work.

The foremost responsibility of any president, above all else, is to guarantee the security of our nation—a guarantee of freedom from the threat of successful attack or blackmail, and the ability with our allies to maintain peace.

But peace is not the mere absence of war. Peace is action to stamp out international terrorism. Peace is the unceasing effort to preserve human rights. And peace is a combined demonstration of strength and goodwill. We will pray for peace and we will work for peace, until we have removed from all nations for all time the threat of nuclear destruction.

America's birth opened a new chapter in mankind's history. Ours was the first nation to dedicate itself clearly to basic moral and philosophical principles: that all people are created equal and endowed with inalienable rights to life, liberty, and the pursuit of happiness, and that the power of government is derived from the consent of the governed.

This national commitment was a singular act of wisdom and courage, and it brought the best and the bravest from other nations to our shores. It was a revolutionary development that captured the imagination of mankind. It created a basis for a unique role for America—that of a pioneer in shaping more decent and just relations among people and among societies.

Today, two hundred years later, we must address ourselves to that role, both in what we do at home and how we act abroad—among people everywhere who have become politically more alert, socially more congested, and increasingly impatient with global inequities, and who are now organized, as you know, into some 150 different nations. This calls for nothing less than a sustained architectural effort to shape an international framework of peace within which our own ideals gradually can become a global reality.

Our nation should always derive its character directly from the people and let this be the strength and the image to be presented to the world—the character of the American people.

To our friends and allies, I say that what unites us through our common dedication to democracy is much more important than that which occasionally divides us on economics or politics. To the nations that seek to lift themselves from poverty, I say that America shares your aspirations and extends its hand to you. To those nation-states that wish to compete with us, I say that we neither fear competition nor see it as an obstacle to wider cooperation. To all people, I say that after two hundred years America still remains confident and youthful in its commitment to freedom and equality, and we always will be.

During this election year we candidates will ask you for your votes, and from us will be demanded our vision.

My vision of this nation and its future has been deepened and matured during the nineteen months that I have campaigned among you for president. I have never had more faith in America than I do today. We have an America that, in Bob Dylan's phrase, is busy being born, not busy dying.

We *can* have an American government that's turned away from scandals and corruption and official cynicism and is once again as decent and competent as our people.

We *can* have an America that has reconciled its economic needs with its desire for an environment that we can pass on with pride to the next generation.

We *can* have an America that provides excellence in education to my child and your child and every child.

We *can* have an America that encourages and takes pride in our ethnic diversity, our religious diversity, our cultural diversity—knowing that out of this pluralistic heritage has come the strength and the vitality and the creativity that has made us great and will keep us great.

We *can* have an American government that does not oppress or spy on its own people, but respects our dignity and our privacy and our right to be let alone.

We *can* have an America where freedom, on the one hand, and equality, on the other hand, are mutually supportive and not in conflict, and where the dreams of our nation's first leaders are fully realized in our own day and age.

And we *can* have an America which harnesses the idealism of the student, the compassion of a nurse or the social worker, the determination of a farmer, the wisdom of a teacher, the practicality of the business leader, the experience of the senior citizen, and the hope of a laborer to build a better life for us all. And we *can* have it, and we're *going* to have it!

As I've said many times before, we can have an American president who does not govern with negativism and fear of the future, but with vigor and vision and aggressive leadership—a president who's not isolated from the people, but who feels your pain and shares your dreams and takes his strength and his wisdom and his courage from you.

I see an America on the move again, united—a diverse and vital and tolerant nation, entering our third century with pride and confidence —an America that lives up to the majesty of her Constitution and the simple decency of our people.

This is the America we want. This is the America that we will have.

We will go forward from this convention with some differences of opinion, perhaps, but nevertheless united in a calm determination to make our country large and driving and generous in spirit once again, ready to embark on great national deeds. And once again, as brothers and sisters, our hearts will swell with pride to call ourselves Americans.